The Mazursky Method:
The Paul Mazursky Interviews

By
Nat Segaloff
Afterword with Jill Mazursky

Author of *Arthur Penn: American Director*
and *Stirling Silliphant: The Fingers of God*

The Mazursky Method: The Paul Mazursky Interviews
© 2001, 2006, 2022 by Nat Segaloff

For purposes of copyright, this edition contains "substantial new material" from the cut version which appeared in *Backstory 4: Interviews with the Screenwriters of the 1970s and 1980s* (CA: University of California Press, 2006) edited by Patrick McGilligan. That copyright was claimed in error by the Regents of the University of California, a mistake that was corrected by documentation confirming the copyright to the Author, who reserves all rights. No part of this book may be reproduced or transmitted in any form or by any means, electronic or mechanical, including photocopying, recording, or by any information storage and retrieval system now known or to be devised in the future, without permission in writing from the author and appropriate credit to the author and publisher. This also applies to Amazon Look Inside® and Google Books®.

Excerpts from non-auctorial interviews appear under a Fair Use claim of U.S. Copyright Law, Title 17, U.S.C. with copyrights reserved by their respective rights holders.

Many designations used by manufacturers are claimed as trademarks or service marks. Where those designations appear in this book and the author and/or publisher were aware of such a claim, the designations contain the symbols ®, ℠, or ™. Any omission of these symbols is purely accidental and is not intended as an infringement. Oscar®, Academy Award®, and AMPAS® are registered trademarks of the Academy of Motion Picture Arts and Sciences ©AMPAS.

Attempts were made to source photographs in this book. Photographs from the Mazursky family (© Estate of Paul Mazursky) are so noted. If anyone feels their photograph has been used improperly, contact the publisher with proof of ownership and it will be removed from future editions.

Grateful acknowledgement is given to the Margaret Herrick Library of the Academy of Motion Picture Arts and Sciences. Thanks also to Jeremy Ritzlin, Ph.D., Ken Kamins, Nico Jacobellis, Donovan and Claire Brandt, with special thanks to Kimberlyn Lucken and, of course, Ben Ohmart and Bear Manor Media. Particular thanks to Jill Mazursky for keeping her father's creative and personal flame alive, and for her blessing on this book.

Segaloff, Nat, 1948 –
    The Mazursky Method: The Paul Mazursky Interviews /

Published in the USA by: BearManor Media
1317 Edgewater Dr #110
Orlando FL 32804
www.bearmanormedia.com

Paperback ISBN 978-1-62933-840-8
Hardback ISBN 978-1-62933-841-5
Book design by: Robbie Adkins, adkinsconsult.com

The Mazursky Method:
The Paul Mazursky Interviews

By
Nat Segaloff
Afterword with Jill Mazursky

For David Kleiler
asa nisi masa

Table of Contents

Foreword ix
A Different Place 1
Direct or Die 15
When Writers Divorce 29
A Man and His Cat 37
Next Stop, An Autobiographical Film 47
It Isn't a Remake of *Jules and Jim*! 65
Three of a Kind 75
Photo Gallery 99
Riding High 111
Isaac Bashevis Singer, A Love Story 123
There Are No Rules 149
No Tricks in My Pockets 163
Epilogue 171
Afterword: Jill Mazursky 175
Appendix A: Paul Mazursky Filmography 181
Appendix B: Unrealized Projects 182
Appendix C: Notable Awards 183
Nat Segaloff biography 185
Index 187

Foreword

No filmmaker of the 1960s, 70s, or 80s captured the sensibilities of American society, particularly its middle class, with as much honesty, humor, insight, and compassion as Paul Mazursky. Especially compassion. From the confusion of people searching for their place in the cosmos in *Bob & Carol & Ted & Alice* to the anguish of one-sided romance in *Blume in Love*, and from the uncertainty of modern relationships in *Willie & Phil* to the shock of losing a relationship in *An Unmarried Woman*, Mazursky's films—sometimes written alone, sometimes in collaboration—are complex maps of the human heart. But not just anyone's heart; his sensibilities were focused on adults, those with ordinary problems, ordinary goals, and ordinary opportunities. In short, the audience. And while he resisted analyzing his writing process, it's safe to say that, in sixteen produced scripts spanning five decades, he mastered it.

Paul died June 30, 2014 at age 84. His last theatrical film as writer and director had been *The Pickle* in 1993, though he made two television films from other people's scripts (*Winchell*, for HBO, in 1998; *Coast to Coast*, for Showtime, in 2003), a short documentary, "Big Shot's Funeral: Paul Mazursky in Beijing" (2001), and the documentary, *Yippee: A Journey to Jewish Joy*, in 2006. As an actor, he continued through the 2011 video short "Jesus Sex Scandal" and had a posthumous credit when Orson Welles' long-delayed *The Other Side of the Wind* was finally completed in 2018.

The extensive interviews for this book were conducted in the latter half of 2001 and were published in 2006 in a greatly truncated form in *Backstory 4* from the University of California Press.

For this BearManor edition the Q&A has been fully restored and updated and, for the sake of intimacy and immediacy, has been kept in time-present as if Paul were still alive. At least that's the way I think of him.

I first had the pleasure of meeting him when I was doing regional publicity for Twentieth Century-Fox (when they still had their hyphen and long before they were engulfed by Disney) and he came east to promote *Harry & Tonto*. Press tours by filmmakers to major cities were relatively common in those days, the middle 1970s, especially with films that the studio felt needed "special handling." Often that meant that the marketing department didn't know how to sell the picture, so they let the actors or directors do it. With *Harry & Tonto*, however, Paul was awash in well-deserved critical adulation and he was a joy to be with. A former actor and sketch comic, he played the press to a tee and helped his film score with audiences.

Film critics constantly praised Mazursky by noting that "he loves his characters," but that's being facile; all writers love their characters—even if the characters behave in unlikable ways—or they couldn't write them. What distinguished Mazursky was that he loved his *audiences*. More than that, he understood them, how else could he consistently create for them such fully realized people who face relatable challenges within a recognizable world—just like the viewer? At the same time, he wondered if his material was sometimes "too hip for the room," a showbiz phrase for jokes that fly over people's heads. And yet, as these interviews quickly reveal, Mazursky never wrote down to the public, he wrote at eye-level and, at his best, tried to elevate them. The room was invariably hipper while he was in it. He was a participant as well as an observer, and he understood the absurdities, the realities, the heartache, and the elation of Life's journey.

Irwin Lawrence Mazursky's life journey began on April 25, 1930 at Brooklyn Jewish Hospital. Raised in the Brownsville section of New York's most assertive borough, Mazursky attended P.S. 144, all the while dreaming about becoming an actor to escape his moody, domineering mother, Jean, and his passive father, Dave (in 1976 he would write and direct a film about it, *Next Stop*

Greenwich Village, casting Shelley Winters and Mike Kellin as his parents "Faye" and "Ben."). On graduating from Brooklyn College in 1951 with a degree in Speech Therapy, he moved to Manhattan where he worked as a juicer at the pre-trendy Salad Bowl vegetarian restaurant. In 1953 a writer friend, Howard Sackler, arranged an audition for Mazursky with tyro filmmaker Stanley Kubrick, to whom he had just sold a script; the result was a starring role in *Fear and Desire* the first film for both. Two years later he was flown to Hollywood to appear in Richard Brooks' trend-setting *Blackboard Jungle*. Neither film led to stardom, however, and he returned to New York to study with Lee Strasberg while simultaneously working in improv comedy, notably as "Igor" of the comedy team "Igor & H," the "H" being Herb Hartig. Engagements at the Village Vanguard, Bon Soir, The Purple Onion, One Fifth Avenue, the hungry i, and other clubs marked him as a rising comic writer-performer. But his aspirations remained in drama.

As his career moved forward, so did his life with Betsy Purdy, a graduate student in Library Science he had met in Washington Square Park in 1952 and married that same year. Their first daughter, Meg, was born in 1957. When television moved to Los Angeles in the late 50s, so did the Mazurskys, relocating there in 1959. To augment his acting income, he began writing spec scripts for episodic TV shows, eventually selling one to *The Rifleman*, which got him into the Writers Guild. Their second daughter, Jill, arrived in 1965.

In 1960 he got a call from former nightclub manager Larry Tucker who had just been asked by Chicago's Second City troupe to open their Los Angeles franchise, and he wanted Mazursky—whom he had once declined to hire as Igor and H—to help him shape a show. At the time Mazursky was working as a bicycle messenger, so he had no problem forgiving Tucker's lack of foresight, and accepted. Within two years the team had joined the writing staff for *The Danny Kaye Show* on CBS-TV, where they stayed until 1966, during which tenure they moonlighted on their own feature script called *H-Bomb Beach Party*, which was sold but never produced. After *Kaye* ended, they developed the series *The Monkees* (1966) and, again on spec, wrote *I Love You, Alice*

B. Toklas (Hy Averback, 1968), which became a hit for Peter Sellers. When they put their script for *Bob & Carol & Ted & Alice* on the market the next year, Mazursky wouldn't sell it unless he was attached as director. Producer Mike Frankovich and Columbia Pictures agreed, and everybody got rich.

Ostensibly a satire on the touchy-feely movement that was then seducing America, beneath *B&C&T&A*'s jokes is a story about how people waste their time searching for gurus rather than examining their own souls. Its gentle but acute perceptiveness set the pattern for nearly all of the writer-director's subsequent work; as David Rosenthal wrote in *Rolling Stone* (October 28, 1982), "a Mazursky film is physical movement. Someone is always taking it on the lam as an answer to his prayers." Certainly that is the trajectory of Robin Williams in *Moscow on the Hudson* (1984) as Russian defector Vladimir Ivanof; Art Carney's Harry Combs in *Harry & Tonto* (1974) who crosses the country; George Segal's obsessive ex-husband Stephen Blume who flees to Venice in *Blume in Love* (1973); Architect Phillip Demetrios (John Cassevettes) who takes over a Greek island in *Tempest* (1982); Richard Dreyfuss who impersonates a dead South American dictator in *Moon Over Parador* (1988); and Michael Ontkean as the peripatetic Willie Kaufman in *Willie & Phil* (1980). It can even be argued that Dave Whiteman (Richard Dreyfuss) ventures into a strange land when he dwells among the homeless in *Down and Out in Beverly Hills* (1986), and Donald Sutherland and Danny Aiello leave reality to work in Hollywood in *Alex and Wonderland* (1970) and *The Pickle* (1993), respectively. Finally, when Woody Allen wears a pony tail and carries around a surfboard in *Scenes from a Mall* (1991), there can be no question that he's not in Kansas—er, New York—any more.

Mazursky also traveled far. "I've had a wonderful journey," he said, reflecting on his rarified status as an independent filmmaker who functioned freely within the Hollywood studio system. "I was blessed. I was left alone by all these people for so many years." Otherwise, though, in our talks he declined to analyze his own work, even though it is rife with characters who go to shrinks to analyze themselves. A writer who insisted that he created intuitively, even with his collaborators, he remained modest about the films he made while bottling his frustration at having trouble making new ones (see Afterword). In the final analysis, the only person who could make a Paul Mazursky film was Paul Mazursky.

Despite discordant tones of personal frustration in our talks, in his on-screen work, optimism was another Mazursky trademark. Even his darkest film, *Enemies, A Love Story* (1989), ends, not with the death and uncertainty that Isaac Bashevis Singer tacked onto the end of his novel, but with a birth. Similarly, *The Pickle* (1993), Mazursky's last filmed screenplay, ends in a re-birth.

Mazursky, too, enjoyed re-birth as an actor. While he always played roles in his own films, he became better known in his later years as an actor rather than an auteur, appearing in such widely varied projects for other filmmakers as *2 Days in the Valley, Carlito's Way, Love Affair, Antz*, and, most notably, *The Sopranos*. Indeed, when these interviews began, he was freshly back from China where he and Donald Sutherland were the only English-speaking performers in *Big Shot's Funeral* (Chinese title *Da Wan*, Xiaogang Feng, 2001), re-pairing them thirty years after they first shared a scene in *Alex in Wonderland*.

Always the actor even when he discussed writing and directing, Mazursky didn't just give an interview, he gave a performance. What follows is often darkly funny and, if there was a word for a raised eyebrow and wry smile, it would be found throughout. When we spoke it was a dozen times between June and October 2001 in Mazursky's office at Tecolote Productions (Spanish for "owl") that occupied three rooms in a non-descript Beverly Hills commercial building. He would arrive there every morning after he'd had coffee and bagels with friends at the Los Angeles Farmer's Market. While his assistant, Kimberlyn Lucken, managed his schedule, Mazursky variously wrote, phoned, and entertained visitors in his inner office, which was decorated with a gallery of family photos, inscribed mementos from Fellini, Mel Brooks, and Woody Allen, and such esoterica as a framed copy of *Mad Magazine*'s spoof of *Bob & Carol & Ted & Alice*, titled "Boob & Carnal & Tad & Alas." The array was both personal and eclectic, much like

Mazursky himself, whose sharp wit and character writing placed him at odds with the youth-driven films being packaged and produced elsewhere in the town he lived in—and poked gentle fun at—over a 61-year career.

NOTE: This Q&A is loaded with spoilers. If you haven't seen the films of Paul Mazursky, come back to it after you have.

A DIFFERENT PLACE

Nat Segaloff: Nearly everybody who writes about your work comments that you "like" your characters, even the negative ones.

Paul Mazursky: I'm sympathetic to them. I always felt that the middle class was not treated equally in terms of tragedy. You had to be very rich or very poor to be thought of as a tragic figure if you fell from a state of grace.

You started writing and directing films at a time when people were just starting to be able to "get in touch with their feelings" and "express themselves," and that formed the basis of your early successes.

You see, the wonderful thing is that, early in one's career, you're not stopping and thinking about "will this be a hit" or "do I have to live up to anything" or "will they like this" or "can I sell this?" It crosses you're mind vaguely, but I never would have made *Next Stop, Greenwich Village* or *Harry & Tonto* if I had worried about a big hit. But those days seem like centuries ago because they worry much more now about "will the kids get it?"

Is it fair to say that when production executives could relate to the theme of a film, the film was more likely to be green-lighted than today when the executives have to consult their marketing people instead of their gut?

You're absolutely right. You don't have much chance now. You'd have to be Spielberg or someone like that to make *Schindler's List*. Don't forget, for me to get to make *Enemies, A Love Story*, which was '89 or '90, I got lucky. Joe Roth read it and told Jim Robinson—they were running Morgan Creek—and they gave me ten million bucks to make this movie. I don't think I could get it made today unless I could make it digitally for like $80,000, 'cause no one wants to see a movie about a Jewish guy who actually speaks Yiddish in the movie and has three wives at the same time. It's a different world. Someone said that they like that nine-year-old range now. We're no longer talking about 18-25, we're talking about *nine years old*! And if you get much past that, it worries them. There's no point in criticizing it. It's a different place.

When did you become aware that films were "written"?

(Long pause) When I became a writer for Danny Kaye—during that period, for four years—I started fooling around with writing movie scripts. I didn't even start to think about writing a movie script. You're obviously aware that they're *written*, but I never much thought about it. I'd always see a movie by a great director and I was always aware that there was a name on it—Nunnally Johnson, famous ones—but I didn't really know that much about the process. Most of what I knew would come from books by people as far apart as Eisenstein[1] and Puduvkin[2], which I read early on when I was in my twenties, and I read them more as intellectual exercises than that I was going to direct a movie. Karel Reisz[3] wrote a wonderful book on editing. John Howard Lawson[4] was a dramatist; he was also a dramaturge. So I was aware of it, but never thought about it much. Then, when I started to write screenplays, I somehow got ahold of a couple and looked at them, and I

---
1 *Film Form: Essays in Film Theory.* Edited and translated by Jay Leyda. NY: Harcourt, Brace, 1949
2 *Film Acting,* translated from the Russian by Ivor Montagu, London: George Newnes, Ltd., 1933
3 Reisz, Karel and Gavin Millar, *Technique of Film Editing,* NY: Communications Arts Books, 1979
4 *Film the Creative Process.* See also *Film in the Battle of Ideas,* NY: Masses & Mainstream, 1953

immediately decided I wasn't going to write screenplays with a lot of directions. All I like to put in is "cut to" or "dissolve to," "fade in" or "fade out," where does it take place, and, if it's important, what time of day it is. And if it's *really* important, is there something in the scene that happens, or something you see that the reader should know about, so that they can get a better picture? But not dense and filled with literary allusions. One of my writing partners, who's very gifted, is Leon Capetanos. Leon tends to put in a lot of description. I leave some of it in, but some of it I take out because most [studio] people don't read very well, so you don't want to get in the way too much by saying that "Jack is a former alcoholic who has seen better times, and his frayed pants. . ." It sometimes helps, and if it does, do it. When did I become aware? When I started to write, I became aware of the writer. Early on in my writing, I wanted to direct. I will say that. Which is interesting.

You had written fifty-odd short stories and scripts for television and the only one you wound up selling was one to The Rifleman and that was rewritten by someone else.[5]

I never wrote fifty. I wrote *The Rifleman* with a guy named Skippy Edelman—Julius Edelman—and wrote it on spec. I'd acted in one of *The Rifleman* episodes[6], so I brought it to Arnold Laven of Levy-Gardner-Laven and I said, "I wrote this thing on spec" and he read it and he said, "Okay, it's a deal." So then I was in the Writers Guild and got paid peanuts. I might have written five or six, seven or eight, I don't know, television shows that I didn't sell, that were for shows that were on, that I'd write on spec. I wrote *The Cara Williams Show*. Of course I wrote *The Monkees*. And then *Danny Kaye* for four years. That's all. I never wrote a lot of television.

There's the story that says you met Larry Tucker when you and Herb Hartig auditioned for him at Down in the Depths night club.

---

5 "Tinhorn" (1962)
6 "Hostages to Fortune" (1963) and also "Shotgun Man" (uncredited, 1960)

He didn't hire you, but later he called you because Second City had asked him to get their show in shape and he called you.

Larry called me. I had auditioned for him in New York with Herb [when] Larry was running a night club, Down in the Depths, and we didn't get it. A couple of years later I moved out here. I get a call from him, he says, "Remember me?" I said, "Sure, you're the guy that didn't hire me." He says, "Well, I've given all that up. I'm looking for an agent." So we started talking, and we were funny guys, and he said, "They're looking for replacements at Second City." So we both took over the Second City shows [in Los Angeles] as co-leaders, and we began to do our own improvs. We did it for six months at the run at the Ivar [Theatre] and then we transferred the show to the LaGrande Theatre for about a year, and then we did another show at the Interlude for Gene Norman called *Wild, Wicked World*. Somebody saw us along the line, and we got the *Danny Kaye* gig. We did four years at *Danny Kaye*, during which we wrote *H-Bomb Beach Party*, which was optioned but never made, and then *Toklas*.

I've read in two places that when Larry Gelbart left Kaye to write A Funny Thing Happened on the Way to the Forum, you and Larry Tucker were hired to replace him because the writing staff didn't consider you to be threats to their jobs.

I don't really think that's quite true. Larry Gelbart had only agreed to do one show, and they very quickly realized that they needed another writer or two. At that point they had Mel Tolkin, Shelly Keller, Gary Belkin, Ilson and Chambers, a team; Herbie Baker writing musical stuff; there might have been another. So the producer, Perry Lafferty—I'd acted for him on *Robert Montgomery Presents* when he was a director—knew me. He saw Second City and said, "Jesus, you're funny as hell. Do you think you two guys. . .?" He says, "I'll give you $340 a week for four weeks. Try it." So it wasn't so much that they didn't see us as a threat—we *weren't* a threat. All the work was done at meetings without the producer there, without Danny Kaye there. We would only see him when we pitched the show when it was already done, so they didn't even pay attention to us for the first couple of weeks. We wrote a sketch or two. Then they ran into trouble with the show about three or four weeks later and said, "Where's that piece of shit you guys wrote that we threw in the garbage?" Well, we had a copy, and pretty soon it was on the show. We didn't get any credit—everybody wrote everything. There was no head writer; the head writers were basically Shelly and Mel, who argued a lot. They were very funny guys. Larry and I were the only ones that stayed the four years. It was a tremendous learning experience where you were forced to come up with something, whether you liked it or not, every week for 39 weeks, and then we'd have this great three months off where I'd go act or we'd write a movie or something.

There's a theory that the reason early television is so highly regarded is that, when it started, only rich people could afford sets, so writers tended to write for a sophisticated audience. But as TVs got cheaper and more people put them in their homes and antennas began popping up in Iowa, they had to dumb the stuff down so it would have broader appeal.

I never heard that, but it's a reasonable theory. I mean, let's face it, the proliferation of what has to be filled in on television—you're now talking about ABC, NBC, CBS, Fox, Turner, cable, HBO, Showtime, E channel, all day long—there's not enough stuff for that. You're basically dealing with common denominator stuff ninety percent of the time, which means: moron. The miracle is that you still get the other five or ten percent. And you've got to understand something else: with all my complaints, and I have a lot, when you think of the BBC, which has got the highest standard I can imagine, even though they produce some soap operas and they're pretty amazing, nobody's making any money. They're getting big stars, the greatest directors, the best talent, the best of everything, and they're working for peanuts. They don't care. They want to do good work. Then, when they want to make money, they come here to whore. Pretty soon they start directing American stuff and their careers suffer. Not all, but most of them.

The first script you and Larry wrote together was called H-Bomb Beach Party.

We were in our second or third year of writing for Danny Kaye, and we wrote a movie about two H-Bombs that were lost off the coast of Spain[7]. This actually happened. Larry and I finagled free tickets to Spain, round-trip, by writing some funny lines for the Woody Allen movie *What's Up, Tiger Lily?* for the company that was behind it and needed some more dialogue. Instead of paying us [we got] two round-trip tickets to Spain. So I had the good fortune to go to Spain—Europe!—for the first time. Just landing at the airport was a high. It was different. It wasn't like a modern American airport.

The light is different, the smells are different—

Everything. We went down the coast near Malaga and found the place where the bombs had been and they had looked for them. We did some research that helped us. And then we made up a place called Maropaulo, which was the poorest island in the world. We begin this movie with a comic documentary about this island (does tacky travelogue narrator voice) "Maropaulo! Jewel of the Mediterranean! Home of Ambergris and the whales! Not a whale has been sighted in sixteen years—they now live on rocks!" And we showed this very funny film. What happen is that we see the bombs are lost, we see the reaction of the American generals, a kind of *Dr. Strangelove* thing. And then we cut back to Maropaulo where a dead whale has washed ashore and he's got a parachute sticking out of his mouth. They find the bomb and they've got to make a decision, because by this time the American army has already sent troops to this island, and the troops

---

7   On January 17, 1966 a U.S. Air Force B-52 bomber and a KC135 refueling plane collided and dropped a hydrogen bomb somewhere off the Spanish coastal village of Palomares. Eight crewmen were killed. The UXB was found two months later. The incident also inspired Ian Fleming's James Bond novel, *Thunderball*.

are spending money. The Maropaulans are making Maropaulan pillows, there's a red-light district, which is now thriving, where the red light doesn't even work. And the priest makes a decision with the people late at night—they look for a sign from God and a chicken cackles—that they're going to hide the bomb. Because if they reveal that they've found the bombs, everything goes away. So they hide it in the catacombs of a church. That's what the movie is about. It's very funny, and lo and behold, a guy named Hunt Stromberg, Jr. bought it—optioned it for like a dollar—and the next thing we know we're told that Laurence Harvey wants to play the lead. He is the lieutenant in charge of finding the bomb, and he falls for the hooker, all that stuff. And we have a fabulous lunch— Larry, Lawrence Harvey, Hunt Stromberg, Jr. and I—at The Bistro[8]. All this is new to me. I'm 35 but I'm not in the movie business. It's our first script, someone's optioned it, Laurence Harvey's a big star, I'm gonna direct. I'm shaking with joy. And the next thing I hear a few days later is that somehow it fell through. That was the end of that.

Sic semper optimist.

But that script *was* funny, and if I had great courage—Larry just died[9] so I can't get him to work on it—it still works, but it needs a rewrite. Anyway, that was number one. Number two was *I Love You, Alice B. Toklas! Danny Kaye* was over. We had gone through 1963, 4, 5 and 6, rented an office on Sunset Boulevard—that was the days when the hippies were walking the streets in costume— and we'd just stand out in the streets and look at everybody. We already had an idea about a Jewish lawyer who drops out and becomes a hippie, but it's too much for him. And we wrote the movie. We were gonna make it low-budget, $250,000. I was gonna direct and Larry was gonna produce. Freddie Fields[10] read it and

---

8   An obnoxiously expensive Beverly Hills restaurant, c. 1960s.
9   April 30, 2001 from complications of multiple sclerosis and cancer
10 An agent, later a producer.

said, "Let me show it to Peter Sellers," and that's how that happened[11].

Everybody writes about the difficulty going from writing sketch comedy to full-length. Neil Simon is the one they usually cite for having done it successfully, but a lot of people started that way.

Woody Allen. Mel Brooks.

Is it just a matter of adding that tenth piece of paper and keeping going?

They haven't all done it successfully. Woody, sure. I think it's a question of going deeper. It's a great word, *sketch*. What does it mean? Brief, quick, five to ten minutes at the most. You "sketch in" characters without trying to get into psychological depths. When you write a screenplay which will last an hour and a half, you've got to get in deeper. Making that adjustment is difficult. I don't think everyone can do it. A lot of writers who have written only sketches never quite make that transition; everything seems a little jokey and unreal. I think I succeeded. I don't know quite how because, I must say, early on I always worried, "Is it funny?" We'd always find the joke, because when you're writing a sketch, you're looking for humor. If you're writing for Danny Kaye to perform it on Saturday, you're praying the audience is going to laugh—not just the six writers on the show.

In your book you go to very satisfying lengths about working for Danny Kaye. You said he lacked irony. I took that to mean that he lacked a sense of humor, that he was a comic actor, but not a comedian.

Danny was a brilliant performer. The "git-gatt-gittle" [delivery] and the dancing and the singing is brilliant. He made you laugh. But he, himself, wasn't particularly funny. If you pitched him very

---

[11] For a full and deserved trashing of the talented, mercurial, and neurotic Sellers, see *Show Me the Magic*, op cit.

odd, offbeat humor he would give you a glazed look: "Huh?" Larry and I used to write a lot of the "Shoemaker" character; Joyce van Patten was the daughter. He loved those sketches. He was warm and he treated me very well, but I knew when I went to him with *Harry & Tonto* years later—when I was trying to raise money for it and I suddenly said to myself, "Jesus, he's rich"—I think he coulda done it. Sylvia Fine, his wife, who had nothing to do with the show, but was a big fan of the script, was at our meeting at his house, and he was saying things to the effect of, "can't there be pratfalls" and "can't he step on a box and hit his head?" I looked at him and I was shocked. Sylvia said, "Danny, this is not a sketch, this is an old man trying to find a place to live." He didn't get it.

Must the part itself be funny, or can an actor make it funny? Otherwise it's Margaret Dumont who doesn't get that the Marx Brothers are ranking on her.

In Mazursky's opinion, there are two things you can't teach an actor. You can't help an actor to have a sense of humor. You just can't. Some have it, like Richard Dreyfuss, who can be playing a very serious scene, but he knows what's funny. Some actors, you can explain it to them till you're blue in the face and they won't get it. That's when you've cast wrong. But if you're hiring an actor to be something that that actor can be that they don't have to be funny and the thing is funny, you're okay. The other thing that you can't teach an actor is to have real intelligence.

Are you stuck sometimes if you need a laugh at a certain point but you know it might destroy character or might send the scene in another direction?

That's been Neil Simon's so-called dilemma. I'm not here to criticize a brilliant talent, which Neil Simon is, but he has sometimes been criticized for succumbing to the need for it to be funny, so that many characters will speak in wisecracky tones. It's all right if *one* does, because that's the voice of the writer, but not *everybody*; everybody doesn't speak in punch lines. My wife (Betsy) is incapable of speaking in punch lines; my wife cannot speak funny. She says some funny things, but she doesn't talk in that rhythm.

Characters must be constructed so that their mouths will say those lines.

Yes, and there are different kinds of humor. If you're writing *Some Like It Hot* you can be much broader than if you were writing *Sullivan's Travels*, which is a brilliant, brilliant movie, and is extremely funny. But they don't speak in jokes.

You and Larry Tucker co-created Hey, Hey, We're the Monkees. Were you going to be regulars on the series if it had followed your design?

I was going to direct seven out of thirteen. That was my deal. I'd never directed, so, for me, it was thrilling. We weren't gonna be regulars, we were just gonna come in every now and again. And then we [Mazursky and producing company BBS Productions] got into this terrible argument about who created the Monkees. The Writers Guild sued [BBS Productions[12]] about the merchandising rights. We ended up getting a credit saying something like "created by." These days if you write a pilot, you created it; there's no other source material. We were told to make, "Something like the Beatles." That was source material, but they didn't want to admit to that.

Bob Rafelson (one of the "B"s in BBS) later made the movie Head which proclaimed how the Monkees were a fabricated group. It turned out, though, that the guys actually could play and sing.

They auditioned these guys and hired guys who could play and sing a little bit. Some were better than others. They weren't bad.

---

12 BBS Productions was formed in 1965 by Hollywood scions Bert Schneider, Bob Rafelson, and Steve Blauner. The success of *The Monkees* fueled their distinguished roster of films including *Five Easy Pieces*, *The Last Picture Show*, *Head*, and *King of Marvin Gardens*.

In the pilot, some of their screen tests are actually tacked onto the end.

I don't even know if it's the real tests, or they shot tests; it's a long time ago. All I know is, when we wrote it, we thought it was amusing, we never thought we were changing the face of television, but in looking at it now, I would say that Larry and I are responsible for the ruination of Mankind in terms of starting an MTV style of very fast cutting, nonsensical cuts, taking you from here to there without any explanation, flipping the screen—stuff we stole a little bit from Truffaut. No one knew that, of course, but in our pretense, and Truffaut, of course, got it from silent movies.

TV was very much proscenium-oriented then and you were breaking that.

Completely. I had never directed a movie, so the thought of my directing seven of the first thirteen was a great opportunity to learn how to direct movies. And it never happened! Life goes on. But, you know, when you're in the right, you really don't have any ambivalence about saying, "Hey, we typed in this show, we wrote 'Monkees'"—I don't know if we spelled it *eys* and they changed it to *ees*—they kept saying, "No, you called it 'The Turtles'." Well, we did, but even if we did, so what? We wrote the show! And that was it. The man-on-the-street sequence (the tease that opens the show) was pure Tucker and Mazursky. It was funny as hell and the idea was that, every now and then, we would repeat the man-on-the-street. But then it was all bye-bye.

After Monkees went one way and H-Bomb Beach Party didn't get made, you and Larry wrote another script, which did.

We wrote *I Love You, Alice B. Toklas*. We would spend four or five hours a day in our Sunset Boulevard office, talking, sleeping, walking. I would be at the typewriter. Somehow we'd come up with a couple of pages a day. See, the way to look at it is that if you can get two or three pages a day—*if*—at the end of fifty days you're gonna have a script. That's only two months. It's not terrible. It's not a year. Then you take another month to rewrite, and then at the end of three months you've got a real first draft. My daughter, Jill, who's a writer[13], spends two weeks on a script. They crank out eight pages a day. I'm not gonna criticize it. Thirty pages a week, in a month they've got a script.

John Hughes supposedly wrote a script in a weekend[14].

Yeah, people do it. There are no rules. I was never able to quite do that, and my tendency was, Different strokes for different folks. But I'd try to get very much into it—in other words, break the back of the idea and get to the 40th page—and then, either with a partner or myself, rent a place in Palm Springs and stay away for a week and do what I would call a marathon where I had no life but this project. I did that with Larry Tucker and we wrote eighty pages of *Bob & Carol* in a week. We used a tape recorder a lot. He'd play Bob and I'd play Carol and vice-versa. I'd already written the first 15-20 pages about what had happened at the Institute[15]. It was a miracle. For *Alex in Wonderland* we used the same technique.

In I Love You, Alice B. Toklas[16] there are some enormously funny lines. At the same time, a lot of the humor comes out of the characters just behaving.

It's got to come out of the situation. If you have a mother saying to her son, "So-and-so died, do you remember him?"
"I think I remember him, Mom."

---

13 *Taking Care of Business* (1990) which Mazursky Executive Produced.
14 *The Breakfast Club* (1985)
15 Bob (Robert Culp), a documentary filmmaker, attends an est-like touchy-feeley weekend with his wife, Carol (Natalie Wood), after which they try to get their uptight friends Ted (Elliott Gould) and Alice (Dyan Cannon) to "open up" and be "hip."
16 A Los Angeles lawyer (Peter Sellers) has a mid-life crisis when he has a fling with a "hippie" girl and turns on with her spiked brownies.

"He had the candy store, you remember, and you fell of the stool and he breathed life into you. *He breathed life into you!* Do you *remember* it?"

Well, the lines [themselves] are not funny, [but they become funny] because he's having an asthma attack. One of the funniest things in that movie—we know he's an ambulance-chasing lawyer to some degree—is when the Rodriguez family comes in for his help, and they're all wearing the neck braces from whiplash, from the grandfather to the little kid. There's about eight of them. There's a great line: they were in a van that hit a car because they couldn't see out the back window.

"Why couldn't you see?" Sellers asks.

"Because the chickens were in the back."

At the same time, the scene has a subtext where Sellers' mother bursts in and reports that someone has died, and the Mexican grandfather thinks it's Sellers' father.

There's a conflict within that, yes. That came out of a wonderful partnership. When you sit down each day to write, you never know what's going to happen. You don't say, "then the Mexican will mistake. . ."—it just sort of comes up. And someone says the funny thing and you bounce off it. One of the reliefs of having a partner, particularly writing humor, is that you have someone to say, "That's not funny." Or saying, "That *is* funny." Whereas, if you are writing by yourself, you have to show it to someone else eventually.

You do something at the beginning of Toklas, which is use a phrase that gets funnier as it's repeated. Sellers asking his fiancée, "Did the earth move for you? Did the earth move for you?" after they have sex.

I think it worked in that picture. I wouldn't advise doing it over and over again. The phrase "did the earth turn" was hot in those days; we were all into Hemingway.

DIRECT OR DIE

Nat Segaloff: You began directing with Bob & Carol & Ted & Alice—*a film which, oddly, got dated and then got undated. It has some elements of sketch comedy in the sense that there are set-pieces, but it also develops character.*

Paul Mazursky: They say about Paul Mazursky, "He loves his characters." And he does. It's one of the things that helps me. If you love your characters and feel affection for them as people, you won't cheapen them too ridiculously. So that when Dyan Cannon is forced to say the word *teetee*, you believe it. You have compassion for her. She's so uptight that it's led her to go to a psychiatrist who's going to probe and find out what's going with this sexually repressed woman who can't call a vagina a vagina, she calls it a *teetee*. It comes out of a truth. Dyan, by the way, never met the psychiatrist; he was my psychoanalyst. There's nothing sketch-like in the opening at the Institute—*esalen*, supposedly—because Bob (Robert Culp), as I did, wants to make a documentary about it. His wife, Natalie Wood, goes because she's his wife, and it ends up that they're the only married couple, and they're forced to make a real communication between each other which reveals that she's deathly afraid of him, that he dominates her, won't let her breathe, etc., and all the people in the room beat the shit out of him psychologically. That all happened to me when I went up to *esalen* with Betsy. See, I went up there because I'd read an article in *Time* magazine that showed Fritz Pearls, the *gestalt* therapist, in a hot tub with four or five patients, clients, whatever you call them, and they were all naked. I said to my wife, "There's got to be a movie, let's go." Well, we went, and that's what happened to us, sort of. I then took it to the next step where they tell the story of their incredible weekend to their best friends, Ted and Alice. And there was the movie. It just flowed. There were endless possibilities, and I believe we explored most of them with tremendous honesty, even though we didn't know how to end it.

The thing we have to believe is that Bob (Robert Culp) and Carol (Natalie Wood), who are hip, would have friends like Ted (Elliott Gould) and Alice (Dyan Cannon), who are straight.

When most couples have dinner with their best friends and go home afterwards, they say, "Why is he always doing that to her?" We do that all the time; you wonder why the marriage is still working. You have great affection for them, but they're different. I mean, we (Betsy and Paul) know very few people whom we go out with who we really are prepared to go away with to Europe for four weeks and rent a villa together. We like them, but they're great for three days; [after] four days, I have a headache. I have great affection for about fifty people in this world, but I don't want to live with them.

The scene in which Bob confesses his San Francisco affair moves through logic and emotion, and then sets up the payoff later when Carol has her affair.

It's brilliant comedy, if I say so myself. There are two lines in that movie which are among my favorites of anything I ever wrote. One is when Natalie says to Dyan Cannon, "I have great news: Bob had an affair." And Dyan's reaction is to go throw up, which is what preceded *An Unmarried Woman*. My other favorite line is where Elliott Gould is in bed with Dyan Cannon and they're ready to go to sleep and they've just gotten the news of Bob's affair, and he wants to get laid, and she's not in the mood. He says, "I think I'll take a walk." She says, "Don't walk, stay with me." And it all leads to her flinging up the covers and saying, "There! Do whatever you want! You want to do it just like that, with no feeling on my part?"

And Elliott Gould says, "Yeah." When I heard the reaction to that line at the only [studio sneak] preview that counted, in Denver, you couldn't hear for five minutes. Five minutes! It was a huge theatre. I was sitting there with the heads of the studio. They were flying off the chair. And when the movie was over, they took me by the arm and said something like, "Thirty-four domestic" ($34 million rentals predicted) which was huge in those days. I didn't know what they meant; I thought it was a wine. Then we have the same preview at the Crest Theatre in L.A. Very, very good, but not quite as good as Denver. You know why? The audiences in L.A. are one-third movie people [who are thinking] "who are these guys? What is this movie? Are they gonna be hits? Is that funny?" That judgmental shit, which is why you never want to have your movie judged by those people. Take it to Denver, take it to Dallas, you'll find out about a broad audience. When we were casting this movie, Mike Frankovich—who was the producer who bought it and let me direct it—suggested Natalie Wood. He came up with the idea of Bob Culp, and we used him. He mentioned this Elliott Gould guy, and we had, by that time, read and met everybody in L.A. We had done *Toklas* and we were hot—Jimmy Caan, Richard Benjamin and Paula Prentiss, who would have been good—but we had lost faith in the role. We thought that there was something wrong with the part; Larry and I had become convinced we'd written Ted like a schnook. Then Elliott walked in. We had never met him. He said about two or three minutes' worth of stuff, and I looked at Larry, and told Elliott, "You've got the part." He said, "Don't you want me to read?" I said, "You don't have to read." I now tested three women with Elliott for the other role of Alice: Dyan Cannon; [psychiatrist and our mutual friend] Jerry Ritzlin's wife, Carol, who was good; and a third gal, who was okay. And Dyan was the winner. She was also an idea who came from Mike Frankovich. The test was so funny—"I want to go to bed," "I want to take a walk"—that Mike did a very daring thing. He decided to show that scene, which I used as a test, to the National Association of Theatre Owners trade convention. They saw it, and the bidding for the movie skyrocketed. And, of course, the test was the first thing I directed. I did a ten-minute take with two coverage shots. You don't get too many long and daring scenes in movies any more. They're all afraid they're gonna go "click" [mimes turning off a TV remote]. My other favorite scene is where Bob finds out that Natalie has had an affair with the tennis pro, Horst, and she thinks Bob's gonna kill the guy, but Bob says, "No, no, there'll be no violence in this house" and offers the guy a drink. Horst is baffled when Bob says, "We have Scotch, wine, bourbon..." and Horst says, "I vould like a nice cognac."

How did you get to direct the film?

When I went in to sell the script, I said to Mike Frankovich, "Larry and I won't sell this unless I get to direct it." He said, "What have you directed?" I said, "Nothing, I made a short, *Last Year at Malibu*, I haven't directed anything, but I've directed theatre, and I'm gonna direct it." "Uh-huh. I'll let you know tomorrow." The next day he called me and said, "Okay, you're on." Just like that.

Bob & Carol was presented at the Seventh New York Film Festival. What are your memories of the event?

[Columbia Pictures] told me the New York Film Festival wanted us to open the festival. They said it was dangerous, but a great opportunity. They felt secure. There was a lot of talk about "it's not a festival movie, it's a comedy, you should have something dark and powerful and serious." But Frankovich thought it was a good idea, and I would do anything Mike wanted. I loved Mike Frankovich; he gave me my shot. We went to New York and we all came: Dyan Cannon, Elliott Gould, Larry Tucker, we have some great shots of the festival. My mother came. She lived in New York. I was terrified my mother would embarrass me. And she pretty much—close to—did. She said to Mayor Lindsay, "This is my big-shot son!" That's all she had to say. I shriveled into a corner. At the festival screening, the laughs were bigger than at Denver. Not only laughs but applause. It must've happened 25 times. The ovation at the end was so staggering that I knew that I would win the Oscar®—there was no doubt about that—not only for the best screenplay, but for the best director. I knew that my career was made and that I would never make anything but giant hits. And then we went to the party, which was right across the way at Lincoln Center. Fabulous. We were flying. People were kissing, grabbing, hugging! Somewhere around 11:15 I saw Jack Atlas, the publicist for Columbia Pictures, walking across the floor with a paper under his arm and a very depressed, head-down look, and I knew right away that the *Times* had bombed us. He said, "I cannot believe it. He cannot have been at the same screening I was at. [Vincent] Canby bombed us." I read the review and I then went to, "I will never win the Oscar®. I have no career. I hate New York. I don't understand anything in this world." I went from the extreme manic to a total depressive within ten minutes. Went to sleep, Sherry-Netherlands, hardly slept. Woke up in the morning because the phone rang at 8:30. I pick it up. "Yeah?"

"Paul Mazursky?"

"Yeah."

"This is Pauline Kael. I've never met you."

"I know who you are. Hi, Mrs. Kael."

"I just want to tell you. I read Vincent's review. You're getting raves from the following people." And she read a list from everybody: Richard Corliss, Richard Schickel, Pauline Kael. It was outrageous. She said, "He's out of his fucking mind." And I fell in love with Pauline Kael! I also learned one thing from that, which I really didn't learn, which is Don't listen too much to any reviews. Listen to the public. I mean it in this sense: I'm very critical of myself. I've made some movies that the public didn't like. They didn't go to them. And if they went to them, they were confused by them, or something. A few times I've made movies that had very different reactions in different places, and there you don't know. Like one of my favorite pictures is *Moon Over Parador*, but it made no money. Some excuses I have, like maybe the studio didn't promote it correctly, but they're always excuses. You never know. Maybe it was too hip for the room, which is what I always figure is possible with the kind of movies I make. But the New York Film Festival experience was important because it showed that you could make a commercial picture that was still worthy of a festival. Why not? It's moronic that a festival should only show movies that are strange, offbeat, and hard to understand.

Some people don't think they're doing something profound unless their rear end hurts them.

But that film has profundity. It's about the sexual revolution which, whether we want to admit it or not, was one of the outcomes of the sixties. People are still confused, but they are now prepared to be less confused because we know from statistics that lots of people are doing lots of things that you never thought they would admit to doing thirty years ago.

Let's address something that I know you've talked about before: despite what some people have insisted, Bob & Carol & Ted & Alice was not improvised, it was scripted.

The whole script is written. Larry Tucker and I improvised to write it. We played opposite parts. He'd take a crack at Bob and I'd be Carol; I'd take a crack at Bob and he'd be Carol. We'd just keep improvising. I rehearsed every single scene except the psychiatrist scenes and the scene with the kid. But every scene between the two and the four, I rehearsed. They were prepared. I didn't rehearse the scene with the tennis pro because I didn't want Bob Culp to meet the guy. But there is no improvisation. The closest I've come to improvisation is when I'll tell an actor who's having a lot of trouble, "Let's rehearse once in your own words. Forget my dialogue." Once in a while it helps them free up a little bit, but usually they'll get back to the script. If the script is "You're a raving maniac, I'll never speak to you again, get out of my life" and I say to say it in your own words [the actor may say], "I can't stand your guts, this is, you're a raving maniac, get out of my life." Sometimes the actor will say something and I'll say, "Let's do it that way." It helps them to get a handle. But improvisation—look, I wish you could have asked this question of John Cassavetes, one of my favorite guys, star of *Tempest* and an old friend of mine. John says he wrote all those scripts. Now, I know there was improvisation in some of them. You can tell that Peter Falk, in some of them, is making up stuff. But I'm never sure.

Robert Altman gets the same rap and I know the stuff is written. But it's one of those things that catches on.

If you rehearse a certain way and cast in the right attitude, you'll get the nuance that appears to be improv.

Let's go to Alex in Wonderland which you first brought to Mike Frankovich at Columbia.

Frankovich agreed to do it, and when we got into early talks to cast it, I could tell that he was bothered by the fact that the opening scene in the movie is a man taking a bath with his four or five year old daughter. It upset him; he thought it was dirty. So I told my agents to approach Mike and ask him if he wanted to get out of it, which they did, and we moved it over to MGM.

You had a very atypical—and I use the word properly—experience with James Aubrey[17], the then-head of MGM.

The story, from the editors on the lot, was that James Aubrey hated every single movie brought to him that he inherited [from the previous regime]: *Brewster McCloud*, *The Wild Rovers*—several that were brought to him. My editor was Stuart Pappé, who's still one of my favorite editors, and we had made an arrangement that we would show it to [Aubrey] two weeks from that day. And we started on the "jack story"[18]: "He says one fuckin' word, I'll stand up and say, 'fuck you!'" We got ourselves prepped and we ran the movie for Jim Aubrey and Doug Netter (distribution). The

---

17 Aubrey, dubbed "the smiling cobra," ran MGM from 1969 until he was fired in 1973, during which time his toxic management style earned him a reputation as the most destructive studio head in Hollywood history.
18 Attributed to Danny Thomas, the joke involves a man who works himself into such a frenzy over whether his neighbor will lend him a jack that the moment the neighbor innocently opens the door, the man screams, "Oh yeah? Well, you can keep your stinking jack!"

lights go on and Jim Aubrey says—and I can see this could be okay—"I don't think it'll do any business, but it's really well made. Congratulations." That was it.

And then they rushed it into theatres for Christmas.

We weren't ready. We needed another month. The sound is sometimes a little raw[19]. But, in my opinion, what we really needed was a couple more previews for me to fiddle around with it. I like the picture, I'm extremely proud of it, I think it has greatness—I'll go out on a limb here—but I think it can use some fixing and some help. But I think it's all there. We had it.

Your acting scene as the studio executive is terrific.

I came in second with the New York Film Critics for best supporting actor! The irony of that scene is that I just repeated the role with Donald Sutherland in China[20]. He plays a director and I play the producer who's making a movie in China. His name is Don Tyler and he's making his version of *The Last Emperor* called *The Last Dynasty* and it's way over budget, and he's an unbearable, egomaniacal loser, and I fire him, and he has a heart attack.

You must have lived through scenes like that where you were pitched several projects, none of which you wanted to do, and been offered lagniappes.

I went through things like it. Nobody ever took a Chagall off the wall, but Larry Tucker and I were offered a Mercedes. I asked, "Is it two Mercedes or one?" It was one. I asked, "How are we gonna do it, split the car?" I was offered many things by many people to take meetings, and I never took them. In a way now I'm sorry because—what the hell? But I've always felt that once you take, you pay.

---

19 Indeed, the sound mix was never finished: dialogue needs looping, room tone is missing, etc.
20 *Big Shot's Funeral* (q.v.)

Is this part of the "green awning syndrome" where, after a director has a hit, they let him make any movie he wants, even if it's a picture of a green awning?

I never had that, although *Alex in Wonderland*, in a way, was a green awning film in the sense that Larry and I didn't know what to write about, so we wrote about not knowing what to write about. It turns out that *Alex* is my 8½, but we were in a position because of the success of *Toklas* and the giant success of *Bob & Carol* where we probably could have said that we wanted to do a movie about a dog that inherits money—that sounds good, by the way—and they would have done anything. When you have 16 children—I call each movie my child—and one has suffered greatly, you love that child more. I think there are sequences in *Alex* that are spectacular. I've showed the movie to Fellini—he's in the movie, you know—and Federico never much discussed my movies, although I know he liked them. I showed him *Bob & Carol* and he told me "delicious, warm, funny. I'll be in your movie." That's why I showed it to him. When he saw *Alex*, he said to me, "Your family is beautiful. Your wife. Your children. You don't need all those fantasies." He told me that. I don't agree with him, but that's the way he saw it. You never know what you're doing when you do it, you just do it, and some things work and some don't. The failure of *Alex* crushed me and I decided to try to see what it would be like to live in Europe where there was Art with a capitol A and the Renaissance with a capital R, and I convinced my darling wife to move to Italy with me and the two kids. I had plenty of money from *Bob & Carol*. She'd never been to Europe. I had a six year old kid and a twelve year old kid. Difficult. We had a very nice apartment and all of that, but I had to put the kids into school, they all got the flu—

Betsy never cottoned to it, either?

Because of all of that, plus the fact that there was a strike almost every day—a *choporo*. You go to get a shave and the guy is shaving you and halfway through he stops and says, "*Scusi—choporo!*" He gives you a towel and you walk out with half your face done. The water, the garbage, the banks, the post office, the museum, the airport, everything went on strike, plus snow in the Coliseum. So Betsy didn't like it. But that's how badly I took the blow of *Alex*. That's where I wrote the treatment for *Harry & Tonto* and got Josh Greenfeld started on it, and out of living there for the four, five, or six months, *Blume in Love* came out of me. So it was great.

How did you get Jeanne Moreau for Alex and Wonderland?

My idea was to use doubles or maybe find other people who were famous. She was in L.A. and I called Mike Medavoy who was one of my agents and I knew that he knew Antonioni. I said, "Do you know where I can find Jeanne Moreau?" He said, "Sure, she's in town. What do you want?" I told him what I want and he called her and then called me and said, "She'd like to meet you. She saw *Bob & Carol*. Invite her over for dinner." So Betsy and I had a party in our house. Medavoy arrived with Jeanne Moreau and I fainted; I opened the door and there's the woman from *Jules & Jim*. Devastating looking. "Hello. . ." I had invited a couple other friends of mine to break the ice. I told her the idea for *Alex*: she'd be walking down Hollywood Boulevard with Donald Sutherland. They met at a book store. She said, "When do you want to do this?" I said, "Any time in April. It will take two days and you will have to fly here." "So it will take about a week?" "Yes," I said, "Do you want to read a script?" She said, "No." That was it. That doesn't happen here. Here you go through six managers, two bodyguards, the agents brigade, a business manager, the wife—who knows? This is why it's so hard to make movies here. See, the artists in Europe, you call them on the phone yourself and talk to them about it.

Alex is a character who is introspective. That doesn't always make interesting drama on the screen. How did you lick this?

I don't know if I did it well enough. I made him a guy who not only constantly has dreams of movies, but he dreams in the style of other directors. He dreams in Truffaut style, in Fellini style—but not in his own style. Maybe I didn't articulate that clearly enough. Introspective? He talks to a tree.

The big challenge in his life is that his wife has looked at a house and wants him to move in there. That means selling out, paying the mortgage, dreaming less—

The biggest commitments you make in your life, in my opinion, are to have kids and to buy a house. Getting married is a big choice; many people get married and make mistakes. But once you're married and you know you're married, the decision to bring a kid into the world is a huge decision. The poor seem to handle that better than the rich. You see a person with six kids, they don't seem to be harried, but you meet the average middle-class person with two kids and they're going out of their mind. Anyway, introspection—he argues a lot with his wife, his kids are making fun of him. I was having those arguments. Hollywood is a hilarious place, which I think I really captured. It was great fun.

It's interesting that, in a film about a filmmaker as auteur, he doesn't seem to have any interest in writing. He wants someone to give him a script.

I didn't want to make him me. I didn't want him to have the vaguest idea. By the way, one of the funny things is that at least three different producers came up to me convinced that I played them. Ray Stark, Jay Weston, and one other guy. I said, "Believe me, it's all of you." At least two of the people I went to see over the years—Dino DeLaurentiis and Jay Weston—I went to see them about something *I* had in mind, and when I left their offices I had five scripts. They were so heavy I could hardly walk. They pitch you everything. And their attitude was, "You don't like it? Fine! But look at this one, too. Maybe you'll find something in the goods that you like." It's a very healthy attitude.

Maybe healthy for them, but not healthy for the writer.

That's why they're producers. They don't get so personally involved that they're in pain and agony and lose sleep. It's the same with an agent. When you speak to your agent and they give you the bad news, "they turned it down, they passed," you think, "Gee, that poor guy is so depressed! I wonder if he's as depressed as me." He's not; he's waiting to hang up and go to the next call and tell somebody, "We sold it for $20,000." Or another, "pass." He or she has so many calls to make that day, there's bound to be some good news. But if they got involved personally in each one to the degree that we would like them to get involved, they couldn't function. The other thing that agents have to do, and I've seen this, is that they get weird calls. There's the story about the very famous director who called his agent at four in the morning from location and said that the hotel had not given him the key to the little fridge in his room. At four o'clock in the morning he called from Europe! "I'm sleeping," the agent said. The director said, "What should I do?" The agent said, "Call the concierge." "Oh. Thank you." I was with a very famous agent who had a thirty minute discussion with a very famous movie star about getting her a Frigidaire for a tent in Africa. I heard another discussion about getting an air conditioner—"Yeah, okay, we'll get one that does. . . yeah, okay, great." They have their *tsouris*. So a great producer isn't just somebody like Sam Spiegel and others who say, "this idea" and "this writer" and "this director" and "this star." They have a vision. They put it together. They're great. But that person can also handle all the other junk. I couldn't handle it. I'm not good at that. I've produced a lot of my own movies and I'm very good at solving all *my* problems, but if I had to solve *those* problems, too, I'd go crazy.

Can you define "personal film"?

I've always been slightly offended by that. Every film you make is personal. This is the Paul Mazursky theory. So when you see a hack movie, it's a personal picture. I didn't write *Winchell*, but to me it's a very personal film. It filled my mind. I've never made a movie I didn't think that about, including *Faithful*. A guy can say to you, "Yeah, I did it for a payday." Well, they did, but they still did it. A lot of very smart guys have said to me, "This is a personal film." I think what they really mean by it is they're getting less money.

Even if you do a project strictly for the money, it's still going to use up the same amount of time in your life as one you cared about.

I would think it would use more, but I know that I'm speaking out of turn here because I've never done it. Maybe it's easier. Maybe you take that head trip and say, "They're giving me five million bucks and it's gonna take me 10 weeks to prep it, 10 weeks to shoot it, 10 weeks to cut it, that's thirty weeks. It'll take me three-quarters of a year, then I'll go on a good vacation. I may have to get shock treatment, but I'll have five million dollars in the bank." Maybe it works, I don't know.

If you had only three things that you could eat for the rest of your life, what would they be?

That's from *Alex in Wonderland*.

In the film it's used as a running joke—sort of facile profundity—but after all these years what's your answer?

Well, I like chocolate chip ice cream. I always have. I like fruit, so I don't know what kind, particularly, but a nice papaya mixed maybe with a little mango. The truth of the matter is, I guess pasta would be a good third. A good pasta with a little garlic. I used to be cheeseburgers but that's over since I had a four-way bypass five years ago. I have a cheeseburger once a month. But it's different now.

WHEN WRITERS DIVORCE

Nat Segaloff: The end of Alex was also the end of your collaboration with Larry Tucker. He didn't have it easy after that, did he? He became very sick.

Paul Mazursky: Very sick. During the time we worked together he weighed between three and five [hundred pounds]. It was beyond obese. When he hit the five mark, around there, I asked him to go to a hospital because he was falling asleep at the dailies. He could hardly walk, he could hardly breathe. We had a year and a half performing in theatre, we liked each other very much, we were not competitive, ever, to Larry's credit, and to mine. Larry was a wonderful man. Then we had the four years on *Danny Kaye*. We had a lot of laughs. Then we wrote *H-Bomb, Toklas, Bob & Carol*, and after *Bob & Carol* we could do anything and didn't know what to do. I basically came up with *Alex in Wonderland*. Larry helped, but it was mine. At the end of *Alex in Wonderland* I had to go away to Rome for a week to shoot the Fellini sequence. When I got back, Larry, who had stayed here, said, "I had a weekend marathon with a therapist. I never had anything like it in my life, Paul. I made some big decisions. I'm leaving Marlene (his wife) and I'm leaving you."

I said, "You want to leave both in one weekend, Larry? Are you sure?"

"Well, I want to do my own stuff. I still love you and all that but I want to be my own guy."

I said, "You know, you can be your own guy and still work with me."

He said, "No, I've got to break."

I saw [what happened as] that he went into therapy and they said, "You've got to find your independence." They didn't say this to me, but it was my reading on it. Maybe it was so he could lose weight, I don't know. So we broke up. Still friendly. And then he had a very checkered career. He finally had the operation to tie up his intestines and lost an enormous amount of weight, got down to 200, but he also lost muscle tone. And the loss of muscle tone crippled him. Eventually he developed so much trouble with it that he had the operation re-done and that didn't help. He did some TV over the years with a partner named Larry Rosen, and maybe some other people. I kind of lost touch with him. He ended up with multiple sclerosis. I went to see him a couple months before he died. He was flat on his back at home, but in a hospital bed, and he had a tube in his neck and he couldn't talk, he'd have to whisper. It was horrible and very depressing. But he still had humor and still tried.[21]

You both issued magnanimous statements in announcing the breakup.

We were very—he wanted to try—for me it was, like, look what I did. Soon after the breakup I wrote *Blume in Love, Next Stop, Harry & Tonto, An Unmarried Woman, Willie and Phil*, and all the rest. I wrote four of those five myself. So it was a heyday for me. But I like working with partners. I did *Harry & Tonto* with Josh Greenfeld. Then I met Leon [Capetanos] and we did four pictures. Then I met Roger [L. Simon] and we've done about three.

After *Alex in Wonderland* tanked, Mazursky, as noted earlier, went to Europe.

I went to Europe because I didn't know what to do because *Alex* had been such a bomb at the box office. I had sort of decided to try to live in Italy for a while, and I had already come up

---

21 Larry Tucker wrote multiple episodes for the TV series *Mr. Merlin* (1981-1982) and *Stir Crazy* (1985-1986) among other episodics. He died April 1, 2001.

with the idea of *Harry & Tonto*. I convinced Warner Bros. into putting up peanuts, $25,000 or something, and I got Josh Greenfeld involved and we wrote the script together. To make a long story short, when I came back from Italy nobody wanted to do *Harry & Tonto*. They said, "We don't want to do a movie about an old man and a cat. You're a great talent, *Bob & Carol* was a huge hit. . ." blah blah blah blah. They were so negative I didn't know what to do. Someone came along and offered me a picture called *The Flasher* and I was so desperate to go back to work—yet so ambivalent—that out of some crazy need, I said okay. It was a black comedy about a cop who was a flasher. The night after I agreed to do it, I woke up in a cold sweat. I realized I didn't want to do it. So I had to call Freddie Fields, my agent, and say, "Freddie, I don't want it." He said, "Well you better call the studio and tell 'em yourself. I don't want to call 'em because I already agreed." I called them. I then got an office at [what is now ICM, International Creative Management] and sat down in a room and had no idea what to do. I just knew I wasn't going to be doing *The Flasher*. And I suddenly had a memory of me sitting in Italy, and I just started to type, I swear, and out of nowhere came this one-line idea that a guy is in love with his ex-wife. And it all fell in. Each day I would write and I didn't know what was going to happen. I had never done anything like that. The jumps in time that I was making, I just made. I didn't think about whether they would understand it. I flashed forward, back, further back, present, and it keeps doing that and by God it wasn't confusing. So I'm very proud of that movie [*Blume in Love*]. A lot of people really liked it very much. But I didn't realize myself till I saw it a couple of years ago how dark it was. All I know was that I wanted to end with *Tristan und Isolde* and they come together. For whatever reasons, it worked, and I finished the script, gave it to my agent—Freddie or Jeff Berg by then—and he showed it to John Calley at Warners. That was on a Friday. On Saturday they called me and said, "When do you want to start?" What I'm saying is that I didn't think out the meaning of what I was writing. I wasn't sitting here saying I'm writing a social comment. I was just writing about feelings. It never happened to me; *Blume in Love* is a fantasy. I'm still married to the same woman after 48 years. But you fantasize.

It is a very disturbing movie, as dark as they come. You're making a movie about a stalker. He only happens to be George Segal.

Not only that, he rapes her. *Bob & Carol* was a satire about all the new age stuff that was coming into American life with large numbers of people who, ironically, are just as large today, who would do anything. They're like people drowning, grasping at anything—whether it's Depak Chopra, if it's est, if it's the Forum, if it's the latest guru, if it's the Mahareeshi, if it's Scientology—America has tons of people who would grab at those things. They want desperately to be saved. They want someone to explain to them, and tell them for sure, it's not what Shakespeare said, it isn't "a tale told by an idiot, full of sound and fury, signifying nothing," it *means* something. *Bob & Carol* satirized all that. By the time I got to *Blume in Love* I was dealing with a whole other subject. It never happened to Paul Mazursky. I had lived in Rome. I had had the Italian experience, the Rome experience. I was not having an affair or anything like it, but my fantasy took me to a place based on a famous actress who caught her husband in bed with his secretary. And this famous actress kicked the husband out of the house right then and there, and never gave him a second chance. He was still desperately in love with her. The other thing was a sexual adventure. Well, in 1990s you can be the President of the United States and do it 25 times and your wife will stick with you; who knows what's really going on? In 1973 or 4 when I did *Blume in Love*, I guess I was fantasizing what would happen to me if I got caught. I would hope it wouldn't be that much. But all I knew was that I loved the irony of a man being desperately, *desperately*, DESPERATELY in love with his ex-wife. And the reminiscences of it take place in the city of love, Venice, where lovers are all over the joint. You can go to Venice with someone you're barely in love with, and inside of a week you're in love again. So the darkness of it came out of a pretty profound examination, if I say so myself, of how marriage is. In marriage people have to learn to accept the good and the bad. It's easy to accept the good, but the flaws, or the things you don't agree with, the problems—and this marriage was a pretty real marriage. He shouldn't have done what he did, but she shouldn't have done what she did. And the way it works out is the way it works out. I got into the head of this guy and I loved the idea—which I did think of around the end of a week—that he'd end up raping his wife. Which was crazy.

We know today that rape was an act of violence.-

It is.

In the film it's portrayed as an act of desperate love.

It's also violent, though. I think it's violent. He made up his mind at a certain point that he was gonna do it, and she didn't want him to do it. You can get into different interpretations that she really did want him to do it. But he definitely raped her. I don't think there's any doubt about it. Then it made it realer that she kept the baby.

And he kept our sympathies after that.

We do. Some magical way.

It's disturbing.

Exactly. If I'd made it like a cute rape—

The kind where the woman pounds on the man's chest in protest and then gets turned on and embraces him?

No. It's a rape.

The moment after Blume (George Segal) has raped Nina (Susan Anspach), her boyfriend, Elmo (Kris Kristofferson) comes in and she says, "He raped me." Elmo's reaction is to first seek

confirmation from Blume before he slugs him. He doesn't simply believe what Nina just said. That's a very unusual choice.

Well, Elmo was an unusual guy. He's based on a friend of mine. This guy was a jazz musician. He played the drums. Somewhere in the sixties he had bad luck—going home from Jersey, I think—he'd done a gig with a guy who was a bass fiddler and they were driving in a little VW with the bass fiddle sticking out the top. He had his bongos. Their tail light or something was shaking and a cop stopped them to give them a ticket, and found marijuana. They went to jail. The bass player was raped in jail, sodomized, and committed suicide; he hung himself. So the Elmo guy changed his name from whatever it was to something like Elmo and, from then on, became a different human being. Completely dropped out of so-called American society, grew a long beard, got out of jail in a year, went his own way, lived in the woods, started to make drums and play music. He eventually moved to Europe. This was the guy I kind of based the character on, one of those real sixties dropouts with good cause for dropping out. Society had failed him and he no longer had confidence in it. So when he finds out that Nina was raped, instead of saying for sure that he believed her—because he knows how horny a guy can get—he wants to know from the guy, "Do you consider it an act of rape?" and Blume did. Yes. So he hits him.

There's a line that Blume has when Nina catches him in flagrante with his secretary in their bed: "I brought my work home with me." That line is both arrogant and honest. Significantly, he's not the least bit defensive.

Look, if you stop and examine it—if you went to get Freudian—a guy who would do that is looking to be caught. I would say that most men who are in affairs, as much as they do every trick in the book to get away with it, want to be caught. Like Gary Condit.[22] I can't imagine he didn't want to be caught. Now that we're hearing the information, there's so much stuff out there that anybody who

---

22 A U.S. Congressman involved with missing intern Chandra Levy, circa 2001.

wanted to do a little investigating would've known that this girl was calling him constantly, eight times a day. You want to have an affair? Go to the Bahamas for a nice, long weekend and take her with you, say goodbye, and that's the end of it. But Blume did it *in his own house!* That's the story that I had heard, by the way, about this famous actress.

There's an easy-going nature to the film despite its underlying emotions; for instance, the way that Elmo and Steven bond in Nina's car while she's at work—

Elmo's not uptight about the idea of being with the guy's ex-wife and knowing the guy. That's no big deal to him. What the hell has that got to do with anything? They're much hipper than the *Bob & Carol* crowd. See, the *Bob & Carol* crowd, everything's based on guru love, which I feel I participated in, but I'm amazed that, today, in the year 2001, it's as big as ever.

People are still following their crystals.

Everything you can name, people are into. The Forum is now the *est* thing. I've always said that the one thing no one can have power over me about is to say you can't go pee. But when you see these guys on television, call the 1-800 number because Jesus needs this money. The patent thievery is so clear that you wonder how could anybody get taken. In my own experience in going to these things—and I only went a few times—they were very moving. I can't pretend it wasn't. My wife started to cry, I started to cry, people said, like in *Bob & Carol*, "Oh, Mazursky, you don't let her breathe," and I said, "I don't let her breathe!" You cry a lot, you hug people, and you say to all these people, "Here's my number, give me your number, we're friends, we've bonded," and you never see them again, ever. Nor do you ever see the guru again if you're smart. Anyway, *Blume in Love* is very dark, it got a lot of praise, it didn't make a lot of money but it did okay. I think they made a mistake, they released the movie within a month of *A Touch of Class* which was a huge George Segal-Glenda Jackson—

and well-deserved—comedy hit. They shouldn't have released this four weeks later because here was another, darker, marital comedy and I don't think the audience knew the difference. It should have been released in the fall, they should have gone for Oscars®. George was great. But anyway.

A MAN AND HIS CAT

Nat Segaloff: Let's move on to Harry & Tonto, *which Josh Greenfeld began scripting from your treatment.*

Paul Mazursky: Josh Greenfeld started the script while I was in Italy. When I came back he'd already done 50 pages of wonderful stuff. Then I kept writing the rest and he picked up and we started combining. It was a very good marriage. The original script was too long—it was 150 pages, maybe more—but I thought it was a great script. We were turned down, I think, twenty-one times. We set a record. Nobody wanted to do it.

You're 71. Harry Coombs is 72. How do you see yourself in comparison to Harry Coombs?

Harry is not a show-businessy guy. Josh Greenfeld and I both wrote it and put a little bit of both of us in him and I have a wonderful wife and have a wonderful relationship with my kids. I was really inspired by *King Lear*. I said that in an interview or two over the years.

How far do you want to take that?

Take it as far as you want. *Lear* is about an old guy who's looking for a place to live, as I see it. It's about real estate.

But he also foments a war among his three daughters.

Harry's relationship with his three kids is not good. Burt (Phil Bruns), the son who loves him, has married a woman (Dolly Jonah) whom Harry is not crazy about. The only one he's comfortable with is the grandson (Josh Mostel) who doesn't talk, but he's pleased that Burt loves him. Harry's got his own problems. The only person Harry is totally comfortable within the movie is Tonto, the only creature. He obviously was very comfortable with the wife who died, Jesse. Harry's daughter (Ellen Burstyn) is like the relationships of many, many people I know. They have a grown child whom they love, but they can't get along with each other. They're oil and water. They never make up, really—ever, ever. They're always at it. The movie's about parents and children. And then at the end, the irony is, with his youngest child, his son (Larry Hagman), Harry's looking for a place to live, and the son also wants a place to live. And Harry says it won't work out, he can't do it. That scene with Larry Hagman was, I thought, one of the best scenes in any movie I ever did. Larry was sensational. I offered that part to Vic Morrow who turned it down because it wasn't big enough.

Larry Hagman hadn't done a lot of work at that point. It was well after I Dream of Jeannie and before Dallas.

No, he wasn't that famous at all. But he was a very good actor. How do I compare me to Harry? I'm very different. I don't know if I'd have the guts to go on a cross-country journey and stay with my kids. It's one of those movies which, now that I've made it, I'm enormously proud of it, and I know that if I went in and pitched it today, I would be put up against the wall and shot by the executives of the Big Five. The thing that Harry is about is the humanness of it, what he encounters in the journey. The journey is the search for meaning to his life. And at the end—I'm getting profound now—the last shot is with a little girl on the beach, and she's making a sand castle. It's my daughter, she's now 35, I put her in it and told her that, when he starts to sing to you, just stick your tongue out at him. Which she did. And Art laughed. And they keep building the castle as the sun is going down. What does that say? It says a lot of things: Life is when you continue to build your castle at any age. And the poor folks from whom that power is taken away are one of the great shames of our society. You've got to understand that that isn't that way in much more primitive societies, or even in China, where I just came from. When you go to the older sections of Beijing, where they have these places called Hutons, and they have these little plazas where they're selling fruits and vegetables and onions and clothes and pots and pans and there's 30 or 40 people dong tai-chi, music playing on some loudspeaker, and younger folks pushing older folks in wheelchairs, and some just walking, and they're taking care of the grandchildren, they are an integral part of the fabric of their society. They are not isolated and alienated. But the first thing that happens to Harry is that they say, "We're taking your house away!" He says, "Fuck you! You want it? Come and get me!" And he does Lear. Now, I didn't know that when I was 40 years old. Not really. It's written out of a combination of me and Josh. Who knows?

"Tonto" is a Native American word for "fool."

That's like *Blume in Love*. A lot of the reviewers compared the movie to James Joyce. Blume/Bloom. I didn't have the foggiest [notion of that when I wrote it] but I accepted it! No, my mother had a red cat named Tonto. Tonto is because I love The Lone Ranger and the red cat. Ah!

The film got an "R" rating because of the "c" word, which Josh Mostel calls Ellen Burstyn.

I think I made a mistake. I think I shouldn't have done it. It would have made a lot more money. It was my own arrogance. I was right—in the sense that [the R rating] was ridiculous—but I was wrong to challenge it to the degree I did and not give the picture a PG-13 so it could make more money. I went before the Board [Classification and Ratings Administration of the MPAA] with Alan Ladd, Jr., the head of the studio, and I pointed out in very specific detail movies that had gotten PG-13. One in particular was *The Black Windmill* by Don Siegel in which a guy is shot in the crotch 13 times. It got a PG-13. You mean to say it's worse for young people to hear "cunt" than to see 13 bullets? And I remember these teachers, priests, rabbis, saying, "Well, cunt. . ." and they kept saying it over and over till they'd said it 50 or 60 times. I said, "Look, folks, we're all still here." I'm sorry I did it and I'm very proud of Alan Ladd, Jr. and I will be eternally grateful to him for sticking by me, but I shouldn'ta done it.

The character of Ginger (Melanie Mayron) is significantly different in the script than in the film. In the script she's an unwed, pregnant girl, where in the film she's just a runaway. At what point did the change happen?

I think the reason was that, as I started to make the picture, I realized that it's loading it to make her that way. She didn't need those reasons to run away. She just wanted to get away from the family that was probably not fun to be with. It happens every day.

The ending's a little different, too. In the script Harry sings to the girl, "You must have been a beautiful baby."

I took that out because he had sung to the cat, and the old Harry Lauder thing was so powerful when the cat dies that I didn't want to have another song. He has two songs to the cat. At the beginning he says (ala Arthur Godfrey), "Who's this, Tonto? Heh-heh-heh, the old redhead."

The Geraldine Fitzgerald scene[23] also reduces me to tears every time I see it.

That's a pretty good scene. It's based on my wife's grandmother, whom I visited [in a home] and she thought I was the husband. So I had this experience of actually being called "Chester." My wife had warned me it might happen and I played along with it

---

23 Harry revisits an old flame who, he discovers, is hospitalized with Alzheimer's Disease and thinks he's someone else she once loved, and they dance together.

the best I could. I never forgot it. When I went location scouting, those scenes were shot in a German old age home in Chicago, one of the most extraordinary places I'd ever seen. I wouldn't want to be there, but I'll tell you what it had. It had normal old age setup, where people were doing work. Outside the window was the cemetery; that's where you ended up. And it had another wing for those who should have been on life support or dead. Walking through that nearly put me out of my fucking mind. I'll never forget when I showed the movie to the studio. Alan Ladd, Jr.—I gotta give him credit; you know, Universal turned down *Star Wars* and Alan picked it up—Alan had the guts to get me the "go" for *Harry & Tonto*. No one wanted to do it. He had just gotten his job as an executive [at Fox]. He said Gordon Stulberg[24] will give you a million if you can get a name in it that will work on TV in case it doesn't work as a movie. So I got Art Carney. But when Alan saw *Harry & Tonto*, I could see, after the screening, damp [he places his finger beneath his eye and traces a tear], this one drop. That scene with Geraldine Fitzgerald wiped him out.

You know, you take the individual scenes and they're sad, but the totality of the film is uplifting. The film could win a Nobel Peace Prize.

Well, Art won the Oscar® which is like the world's way of saying that miracles can happen. Whoever dreamt that he would beat out Dustin Hoffman that year? There was almost no advertising. They only had five or so prints to show when he won the Oscar®—you know how you get bookings afterwards. I spoke to Art about six months ago. He said, "When can we do a sequel?"

Did his acting ability allow you to drop certain lines and convey them with just him?

I don't remember, to be honest with you. All I know is that anything he had to say in the movie, he never sounded like it was acting. He may have eliminated a line here and there. For the

---

24 President of Twentieth Century-Fox to Ladd's Sr. VP in Charge of Production

most part it's the utter simplicity with which he did stuff. There's a scene where he's driving with the cat in a car. We put the cat on the dashboard and, for some reason, the cat stayed there. The car was being towed [by the camera car during the shot] and Art's there and the cat's there and Art's talking, "You know, Annie was a wonderful swimmer, and I remember once. . ." and every now and then the cat would [does a yawn] and Art never said it like, "I'm talking to a cat." I never directed Art Carney; understand that. The only thing I would do was tell him where to stand or something very simple and basic. He would ask me sometimes, "Do I have to say this?" and we'd cut a line out.

You cut your own scene down, too. [He plays a male hustler]

I'd had enough of it. It was inside. I wanted to show that Harry's encountering a whole new world on the west coast. There's other old folks in the movie. At the chess table there's an old guy talking about the air. His name is Anatole Winogradoff. He's about 90. Then there was Sally Marr, Lenny Bruce's mother. And Chief Dan George[25]. He didn't know any lines.

He always seems kind of spaced.

He is spaced. He doesn't know lines. He just talks. he says, "What are you in for?"
Art says, "Peeing."
"Oh?"
"Yeah, I was peeing in front of the Sands Hotel. What are you in for?"
"Shittin'."
"Shittin'?"
"My horse took a shit in the lobby of—." He's reading cue cards! One of the greatest performances in the movie is this: here I have Ed Norton from *The Honeymooners*, but I don't want him to be Ed Norton, you understand. Now we come to Vegas where he sits

---

25 When Harry relieves himself behind a potted plant at a Las Vegas casino, he is arrested and thrown into a jail cell with the Chief.

down at the bar and he has a few drinks in him before he goes to gamble. I wanted to get Harry drunk. And I've got Art Carney, the greatest portrayer of drunks in human history. The greatest. All I said to him was, "Art, give ma a couple moves, will you, while he's watching these girls?" And if you watch the movie you'll see him do. . . [Mazursky expertly mimes Ed Norton preparing to pick up a drink with a series of well-known hand and shoulder movements for which there are no suitable English verbs]. I'm very proud of the Academy for recognizing him. And you know what pisses me off over the years? Here I've directed all these movies where the *actors* got nominated! *Enemies,* I got Anjelica Huston, Lena Olin. I've got Art Carney, Elliott Gould, Dyan Cannon. I never get nominated as a director. Ever. I was nominated as a writer many times— but as a director, they think I have nothing to do with it.

Josh Greenfeld wrote a book called The Return of Mr. Hollywood about someone who is not you but who is—

[Tensing] It's negative. It's hateful. I haven't read it in years. This is the big falling out we had. We're friendly again, but—I don't think I want to even bother talking about it. It's to no one's advantage.

He mentions your name in passing in the book to make it appear that it's not about you.

Yes, but it's clearly about me.

(Pushing) Was it the result of a falling out at the time, or was he just keeping busy during the Writers Guild strike?

No, no. I'll tell you what it was. After we did *Harry & Tonto,* Josh went from being an unknown writer of magazine articles. He'd interviewed me for *Look* magazine[26]. We'd known each other in college. And while we were doing the interview I said to him, "I got an idea for a movie. What would it be like to be 70?" Josh is a little older than me, and we started thinking about it. I moved

---

26 July 4, 1970 issue

to Rome and wrote the outline of the story, made the deal with John Calley, got 25 Gs, I sent it to Josh, and he agreed to take a crack at the first draft. I gave him, I dunno, 15 or 20 and I kept five because I had money from *Bob & Carol*. We wrote *Harry & Tonto*. It was a great success. It was a wonderful thing. I then got an idea for another movie which was called *Chateau Hollywood* about people who come to Hollywood for miracles. They want to be young, they want to be stars, they want sex; some of them come and they want God. Josh had an autistic child named Noah. Severely autistic. In the draft he wrote, I had urged him to write about Noah, but only one little section. He wrote a screenplay which had a lot about it. It wasn't acceptable; nobody wanted to do it, nor did I want to do it. It had some wonderful things in it and we were calling it *Hallelujah, Hallelujah*. When it didn't work, he wanted to take the script himself, and I said he couldn't do that because all the other things in the script were mine. "I paid you as a writer. You got well paid." I said. "if you want to write about Noah, you should write a book about him." He then went and wrote a book called *A Child Called Noah*. It's a masterpiece. But from that day on we were sort of on the outs. Then he wrote that so-called book which nobody read and it was not a success. But we've made up. It's over. Life goes on.

The book's main character is Larry Lazarsky. He has a kind of redemption at the end, mostly by the goodness of Fate.

You know, I haven't read it in years, and when I did, I read it quickly, and I was so upset by it, I couldn't believe he'd done it. But he did. It's okay.

I can imagine your teeth were gnashing.

If it had been a big hit I might have been upset, but nobody read it.

When you start writing a script with a premise such as "a man wants a place to live," as you did in Harry & Tonto, are you so formalistic that every scene must relate back to that central thesis?

No. What I like is surprises. I like the idea that Harry talks to his best friend, Jacob (Herbert Berghof[27]) about the old days, and he says, "When's the last time you had sex?" and his friend says, "Saturday night March, nineteen fifty-one Yeah, about ten o'clock at night." You get to like the guy, and the next thing, Harry's son is taking him in his car on a rainy day to look at Jacob in the morgue. I don't tell you the guy's dead, you only find it out when you get there, okay? Now, I was in London with my wife and kids and got a call from a friend that my mother had died. I had to fly back to New York, go to the morgue, and identify the body. Same way: they bring it up on a little elevator. So I had had the experience of identifying a body in a morgue, the experience of the person next to me, the attendant, saying, "You want to be alone?" "Yeah." And you're alone for a minute, two minutes. I take real things that happen in my life, and change them and put them into films. That had nothing to do with finding a place to live, but it had to do with [the fact that] his friend was gone. The only friend he really had left now was Avon Long[28], the building janitor, whom he writes a letter to later. I was dealing with real, personal stuff, which is what made my movies unique. They're my view of life; they're very personal. But it doesn't mean shit because John Ford is one of the great filmmakers and I'm not sure how personal *Stagecoach* or *The Searchers* are. I'm not putting it down and saying I'm better 'cause I'm personal, but most of the movies I see now, the most personal they get is *Blair Witch*. They're not dealing with their lives or, if they are, I'm not getting it. With *American Beauty* I can have criticisms but they got into something there—Alan Ball's point of view about a lot of things—and that's what makes it special. You know, I took a scene out of *Harry & Tonto* and for the rest of my years I'll regret it. When I went to the Grand Canyon to shoot there was

---

27 The great actor, director, and acting teacher.
28 Former Cotton Club performer-turned-actor, famous as "Sportin' Life" in the 1942 Broadway production of *Porgy and Bess*.

a big snowstorm, and I have fabulous footage of Art Carney and the cat, and he's throwing snowballs out there and talking. When I screened the movie it seemed a little long, and I cut it out. It was a terrible mistake, because it was very rich and important.

Put it in the DVD and do a commentary.

If I could find it, I would. Among the cognoscenti of cinema I'm highly thought of, but when they talk about that group of the 70s, I'm sometimes in it and sometimes not. They'll say Bogdanovich, Altman, Scorsese. My stuff was more personal than all of theirs, frankly, more a record of Americana. For twenty years I did that, and there's no question there's something there. But it's like, when you get to be 71, which I am, and you're a funny guy, which I am, and you've watched many around you not be aware of the fact that they were getting older and maybe it's time for them to hang up their jock straps, it's very hard to have that same feeling. I don't have any objectivity. So when [the film companies] turn down the projects I've brought them in the last seven or eight years—*Pictures of Fidelman, Down and Out in Beverly Hills, Part 2*—whatever they were called—you start to ask yourself, "Were they turning them down because I'm old-fashioned and out of date? Are they turning them down because they no longer want to make character-driven movies? Are they turning them down because they're morons?" And all those answers have possible truth in them. But they still make movies, and every now and then something good comes along—usually an independent—and I'm even having trouble getting an independent one made. It's hard to keep going and having the, let's say, perseverance to say, "You want to do this?" And the guy says, "We like it very much, but if you can get Brad Pitt to play the old man, we'll do it." It's been very tricky. I'm still offered stuff, but what I'm reading, I don't like.

NEXT STOP, AN AUTOBIOGRAPHICAL FILM

Nat Segaloff: Next Stop, Greenwich Village *is your avowed autobiographical film. When did you decide to do it?*

Paul Mazursky: I had written about 30 pages of it before *An Unmarried Woman* and I was very uncertain and I showed the first pages to Josh [Greenfeld] and he said to keep going. I was like, "Who's gonna want to go see a movie about. . .?" *Next Stop Greenwich Village* took me three months to write and I was shocked when they said Yes. Alan Ladd, Jr. [who was running Fox at the time] was not Jewish—and I mention that because it's obviously about a Jewish guy in New York—his parents, Brownsville. And while I changed some of the stuff, it was kind of autobiographical in that he winds up getting a job in Hollywood like I got *Blackboard Jungle*. I was [also] working in a health food store. It was a lot of fun to write. Over the years I sometimes don't know the difference between using material out of my life or making up material because, after a while, even if it happened to you, when you write it, it becomes fiction. It's no longer you.

But it's real.

I remember vividly the reaction to the movie when it came out. It was not great until Pauline Kael called it a masterpiece. She used the word in her review. I was overwhelmed. I needed that needle in the arm of energy and joy, getting the approval of a great critic, because it hadn't been forthcoming. John Simon said the kid's (Lenny Baker) nose was too long, all that stuff. Then I went to Cannes with it and I remember, at the screening, the audience started to stamp its feet. I was sitting with Shelley Winters and I thought, "Let's get out of here! They hate this movie!" and she said, "What are you talking about hate? That means they *like* it." They stamped throughout the movie. The first time they heard Dave Brubeck, you couldn't hear the dialogue. We got a massive ovation. So here was a perfect example of two reactions to the same movie: the American reaction, which was, "Yeah, maybe it'll work for a month at the lower East Side art houses" and in Europe it ran for a year.

The film is rich in its evocation of the recent past.

The people are all based on people that I knew, but they're composited sometimes. Obviously the mother and father (Shelley Winters and Mike Kellin) are my mother and father. The guy who owns the health food store, [played by] Lou Jacobi, is a vague version of George Haynes, for whom I was the juicer at The Salad Bowl at Broadway and 57th, across the street from the Stage Delicatessen. Ellen Green is based on my girlfriend who cheated on me. Chris Walken is Howard Sackler who wrote *The Great White Hope*. Dorie Brenner is a guy I knew very well. The gal who kills herself (Anita; Lois Smith) is based on another gal I knew very well, named Barbara. The black guy (Bernstein; Antonio Fargas), was a composite of a couple of people I know, but I knew a homosexual who was funny and tragic. That was our "gang," sort of. We often discussed, to great music in cafe, everything that was going on. Arts, literature, politics. We thought we were far out and wonderful.

Anita's suicide is a very complex scene dramatically. You know it's going to come at some point, but you have it turn on a dime so many different ways without ever showing it.

The woman never actually committed suicide. She *threatened* it, as the woman in the film does, several times, and we always used to run over figuring she did, and she never did. But in the movie I give her the business. The movie was a big hit in France, Latin America, Germany—Latin America they named cafes after Cafe Bohemia with pictures from the movie on the wall. The movie was only modestly reviewed in the United States except by Pauline Kael who called it "a comic masterpiece." When we played Cannes, we got a 15-minute standing ovation, and the only ones there were Shelley and Alan Ladd and me. To this day I will regret that they didn't have the money to spend to bring Lenny Baker[29] there, the kid who played Larry. He should have been there to see the reaction of the movie. I don't place too much credence of festivals, although they're very exciting, but the reaction to that movie was overwhelming. They were banging their feet and screaming and shouting.

Very few films have managed to show the compulsion that drives actors to do their work. Fellini has managed to show it.

The acting scenes were what it's really like to take acting, and they were daring in terms of the amount of time spent. They're long scenes. In today's market they would have told me to trim it down to a minute. But we have long scenes where they're talking about Clifford Odets. Then, of course, some of my favorite stuff in the movie was the dreams of the boy with Shelley when she's tap dancing and they kiss. That's right out of my brain, some hot, burning thing I have about me and my mother.

---

29 Lenny Baker died of cancer in 1982 on the brink of stardom. There is a story that goes with it that doesn't directly involve Mazursky, although he is part of it; it's really about Hollywood. When he was casting for the lead in *Next Stop, Greenwich Village*, Paul and his wife Betsy were in New York scouting young talent. I was working for Twentieth Century-Fox in marketing and, at a Friday staff meeting, one of my colleagues suggested that Paul ought to see a particular actor who was appearing in an off-off-Broadway showcase. Paul agreed to go, and a call was made to leave comps for the Mazurskys. On Monday, we asked what Paul had thought of the actor. "He didn't see it," reported the man who had made the recommendation. "My girl called, but when Paul got to the box office, they hadn't put up the tickets, so he left. He never saw the kid." "Well," said another publicist, "there goes that career." The coldness of that comment, even as sarcasm, continues to chill me.

We should probably state for the record that the scenes that look improvised in the acting class were, in fact, scripted.

Right. Michael Egan—who plays "Herbert" in the film, is an acting teacher, by the way. I didn't want to use Herbert Berghof.

Larry's grandmother escaped from Poland in a potato cart and soldiers stuck bayonets into it.

That's my grandmother Ida.

Between the script and the film, you put closure on the scene with Jeff Goldblum by firing his character.

He was great. He was totally unknown. (Doing Goldblum) "Oh really? Oh really?"

Do you direct Shelley Winters or just kind of aim her?

You direct her. You get tough with her. Have I told you how she cries?

No.

She can only cry if you do the following: you have to get a tape or a disc of *Madame Butterfly*, one of the arias. You then put it right next to her chair. She hits the button that starts it. [Mazursky sings] "Oooooooooh, poor butterflyyyyyy…" She hears it and she starts to cry, and she pushes the stop button and says, "It's good, go ahead." As soon as you're ready to do it, she cuts it off, but she's crying. She can do that all day long. That's a fact. I love her. I really do.

When she's in a scene with, say, Mike Kellin, what do you do if they each come up to performance level at different times?

Mike was a consummate actor. He knew he was playing a man, my father, who rarely said anything and was cautious about opening his mouth because he might start my mother off. Mike handled that aspect of it very well. You know, when you're directing great actors there's not much you have to do. Just make sure the camera's pointed at them.

When you were writing Next Stop what did you feel you had to put in to help the audience understand the year and what these kids were trying to do?

The information is inherent in the script, such as the way they dress. Don't forget, the movie was made in 1975 and we were talking about 1953. This is 20 years later. Pretty different. The kind of parties they had, I have never seen since in a movie the subway party that they had in Larry's apartment. All those things are an example of the time. If you'll notice, there's no marijuana in the movie. They're all drinking beer. Abortion is a monstrous, huge thing, and I thought we handled that very well. The use of condoms and diaphragm—all of that stuff is the period. I don't have to tell you more than that, it just shows you how different life was in the late 40s and early 50s in America. Then there's the art direction. If you're doing a movie in New York set in the early fifties, you have to take out the air conditioners, the television antennas, change the signs, make it work, and with very little money. That movie cost about $2,200,000. I wrote *Next Stop, Greenwich Village* after[30] *An Unmarried Woman* and I showed Josh Greenfeld, with whom I had written *Harry & Tonto*, the first 30 pages or so and said, "Am I crazy to be fooling around with this?" And Josh said, "Just keep going. There's something good here." And it helped me.

You needed someone to tell you—

— someone to tell me, "You're not out of your mind doing a movie about yourself when you were 20 years old with your mother

---

30 Though it wound up being produced first

geshrying." You know, when you touch things that happen in your own life, you have no objectivity. I must say, as a writer, that objectivity is bullshit. I always hear "You should be objective." Why?

Well, in the case of Next Stop, approbation for the script was also approbation for Paul Mazursky's life.

That doesn't make a difference. It either works with an audience or it does not. And if you worry about being objective about it, you're not going to do any good, because you're just writing. If you have a partner it's a little easier. It should be.

An Unmarried Woman *is about an upscale wife, Erica (Jill Clayburgh) whose world falls apart when he husband, Martin (Michael Murphy) leaves her and their daughter (Lisa Lucas). Eventually she falls in love with an artist, Saul (Alan Bates), but that's not the end of the story.*

A woman friend of ours named Carolyn came by the house one day. I was living in LA, she was a divorced woman, and she was very proud because she had just bought a first house. She showed me the papers and it said, next to her name, "an unmarried woman." I said, "Jesus, I never saw 'an unmarried *man*.' You mean you're labeled?" And I started to talk to women who were no longer married; I interviewed them the way you're interviewing me. I asked them what it felt like, memories of it, and I came up with this story. I wrote the story out as a one-line outline: "Erica and Martin jog"; "Erica and Martin take the kid off to school"; "Erica fantasizes by herself that she's dancing the ballet." I just wrote lines down. When I wrote the script, some of them became scenes, and some of them didn't work, as is usual. I wasn't sure how I was going to end it; that made me nervous. I just knew that she'd meet a guy (Bates) who was fabulous and she'd turn down his request. But then I thought of this thing—which, I must say, nobody believes that I thought of—which was, at the end, he'd give her a big, huge painting, and she'd be walking down the street holding the painting, with the wind blowing, and instead of putting it down or asking for help, she held onto it herself. She's on her own.

Some films begin with characters who are interesting and you see what happens with them ("character driven"). In others, the writer has an idea and then finds the characters who can articulate that idea by their conflict ("plot driven"). What is your process?

I never think about any of that. I just try to figure out what's gonna happen next—where am I gonna go with the story. With *An Unmarried Woman* I sort of remember that I got her to the pole out in the village in SoHo where she throws up—which was a very powerful moment; audiences were shocked and I was a little nervous if it would work—and it destroyed people. She gives the true, visceral reaction to the news rather than an intellectual one. *She vomits.* The next cut, she's with the four friends and they're all talking about being unmarried. So it was a delightful cut.

And it made the audience care about her 110 percent.

Right. I remember when the movie was previewed the first time in San Diego. Alan Ladd, Jr. and Gareth Wigan at Fox—who were very supportive of me all those years—were nervous because one or two people got edgy and walked out during the scene that Jill Clayburgh had with a female psychologist. All studios, if anyone writes on just one card, get nervous and say, "Maybe you ought to cut X and Y." So I took the scene out and ran the movie for myself, and it was not the same movie because the information that came out during the psychologist scene was more overwhelming than I had known. And I said, "Fellas, you gotta have patience. They're not gonna leave because of that scene." And I was right, thank goodness.

Did you know that *An Unmarried Woman* was going to fire the first feminist shot in a major American movie?

No. I've never known anything I've done would be important. With *An Unmarried Woman* the only thing I knew was that I was getting a lot of resistance getting it financed because of a certain—and I'm not saying this just in retrospect—*squareness* about what was "appropriate" in a movie about a woman. One executive at United Artists—it was a woman executive—even said to me, "How can she *not* go off with this guy?" They didn't know it was going to be Alan Bates, by the way. And I said, "But that's the whole point of the 110 pages you've read. If she goes off with him and does his bidding, she's right back where almost every woman in this country is: in the end you do what the guy wants you to do. The whole point of the movie is not to hate men, not to dislike men—you can love a man, but you love yourself too—and there comes a time in life when you've got to make difficult decisions where you have to do what is right for you at that time. I had this conversation with Jane Fonda, who was the first person offered the part. Jane Fonda said to me, "I want to do something a lot more political than this. If you're interested in me, follow me to England where I'm gonna do *Julia* with Fred Zinnemann, and explain it to me; I don't get it." In so many words, she said that. I said, "Jane, if ever you did a political film, *this is it!*" So I knew that much. But the difficulties were so overwhelming in getting it made that I never stopped and said to myself, "The reason I'm having difficulty is that I'm hipper than the crowd, this is a feminist thing, this is gonna shoot off the cannon." I never thought that. I just thought, "The schmucks don't get it." Jane, by the way, called me after the movie came out and said it's a great movie, she made a mistake, she should have done it, congratulations. I said it's wonderful of you to call me, and I meant it. I liked her very much, still do. I had written the original script for Alan Ladd, Jr. at Fox where I had already done several movies. They were nervous about it because, at the time, they had, in the can, Altman's *3 Women*, *Turning Point*, about women, *Julia*, with Jane Fonda, about women, and they were afraid of another woman's picture. I was very upset and I went to every studio in town and was turned down by everybody except Columbia where Stanley Jaffe read it and said, "I love it, I want to do it, but I want to co-produce it with you, I want to be the producer." I said, "Okay, if that's the only way I can get it made, I'll have a producer." And he was a nice man. But just when we were getting ready to start pre-production, he was fired and David Begelman took over. David Begelman had been one of my agents who helped get the script to Stanley Jaffe! Well, guess what David Begelman did? *He passed.* With no excuse. I thought that I was now in *Alex in Wonderland!* It's at that point that Josh Greenfeld, who had written *Harry & Tonto* with me, called up and said, "Hey, are you aware that Fox is flush with money because *The Omen* opened big?"

I said, "Really?"

He said, "It's in the trades today. You ought to go down."

So I called Alan Ladd, Jr. and said, "Laddie, is there any chance that we can renew our talk about *An Unmarried Woman*?" and he said, "C'mon down." I go down there and I meet with Laddie and Gareth Wigan and Jay Kanter, I think, the trio of executives. And they said, X-Y and Z, and they said, "Can you do something to shore up the character of Martin, her husband?" and I said, "You're absolutely right." So I went and wrote about three lines that weren't in the original, I tore out the first page, waited a week, put a new date on it, and sent it in as a total rewrite. They read it and said, "It's a go." You can print that.

What were the changed lines?

I can't even remember.

The scene where Martin confesses his affair and cries is very effective. It takes a gutsy actor to play that weak on the screen.

It takes a gutsy actor and it takes a gutsy director because, remember, I'm a director who tends to rehearse a lot, and I chose never to rehearse that scene. I was shooting outdoors. They were to come from a scene in a restaurant, turn a corner, and walk down the street. I said to Michael Murphy, before he did the scene, "All I want you to do, Michael, is make sure you cry when you tell her about this thing. I'm not telling you how to cry or what to do, but physically you've got to stop at this point so I can move around you with the camera." And I told Jill, "When he tells you, you can't step farther back than this because you'll be out of the shot." That's all. And on the first take (snaps fingers) he got it. I did it about three times and covered them. And that was it—off to the races. And the last shot in the scene is with a hand-held camera, without a Steadicam—we didn't have Steadicam—where we put cereal in her mouth and I walked down the street with her in a kind of circular move, and she ends up at the street corner and throws up in one shot. My trick with one-shots, which I've always believed, is that by not cutting, you give a reality. There's no rule; you can cut twenty times and give a greater reality; but in my mind *not* cutting made it real that she threw up.

This is the syntax of film.

Yes. In *Enemies, A Love Story* I have a sex scene between Lena Olin and Ron Silver. He and Lena come into a bedroom, they shut the door—the mother is in the other room—and it's silent. You don't hear one word. You hear the El train, and he starts to kiss her and grope her and he picks up her skirt and he takes her onto the bed and he gets her dress off and begins to pull her brassiere off, and suck her breasts, and the camera gets closer and closer—it was hot. In fact, just telling it to you, I'm getting moisture.

Lisa Lucas, the daughter, is quite thorny and has a real edge. When Saul (Bates) tries to be nice to her, she snaps at him, "I have a father!"

Lisa Lucas is a very good actress and a complicated gal. I wanted somebody terribly bright. That was Lisa. She later went to Paris and got involved with a chef. Two of my actresses went to Paris; Molly Ringwald ended up in Paris, and then Lisa. Well, it's a complicated movie.

Then Martin comes back later and tries rapprochement—

That's a real "man" thing: "Take me back," figuring she will. Like he's got a shot! I'd be too embarrassed! I was real good at sympathizing with women, and where I got that from, I don't know.

Throughout your films you have richly developed female characters.

I've been married 48 years. I have two wonderful daughters who are now 42 and 35. I have three granddaughters. I've known a lot of women. I had a very difficult relationship with my mother. But for some reason I find that, in general, in life, talking to women has more honesty. We tend not to talk about how many runs somebody batted in, stuff like that. We tend to talk more about where they're at emotionally and what's going on. There's less small talk.

Watching Erica getting together at bars with her clutch of women friends, one sees where Sex and the City might have come from.

(Laughs) My wife had those women's groups and they always seemed wonderful because they were, again—guys will start with, "She left you? Forget it, you're gonna be fine, DiMaggio hit 54 straight..." They don't want to talk too much about that. "I spent 90 bucks at the Palm!" I'm the first one to admit it. I'm no better. With guys that's the way I am.

Is it that different for you, writing from a woman's point of view?

I don't know now. I haven't written a script in a year and I'm not sure how I'd write about a woman now. I probably should write about an older woman. If I had courage right now I'd write another movie about old age now that I'm 71. I don't feel old, but I wrote Harry & Tonto when I was 40. Now I'm in another place. A lot of what I wrote in Harry & Tonto I think is accurate. And I've just written with Leon—he wrote the script, it was my story, but I contributed a lot—a script about this 90-year-old actor named

Iron Eyes Cody[31]. There's a lot of old age in that. We'll see if it ever gets made.

Erica (Jill Clayburgh) is very hard-edged after she gets dumped. How far did you feel you could take her being resentful or Martin and telling strangers to fuck off before she lost the audience's sympathy?

I wasn't worried about her keeping the audience's sympathy. I never worry about keeping sympathy. I just knew that if the actress who played her was truly likable that you'd have a hard time hating or disliking her. Jill Clayburgh was, if I may say so, the perfect choice. It's hard to think of somebody else playing that part. It was the perfect part for this lady who is, by the way, extremely bright, extremely together, extremely warm, a wonderful actress, attractive in a very realistic, non-Hollywood way, and when she danced in her underpants and did the ballet—which I give myself credit for inventing—I think she won the hearts of everybody. One of the bravest things in the picture is the first sexual encounter she has when she goes down to SoHo and meets Cliff Gorman, who is brilliant, and in the dark, shot by Mr. [Arthur] Ornitz, as she takes her things off, and her breasts are showing, Cliff took a nipple in each hand and pulled her towards him, and she went with it. That was courageous acting.

The film is designed stunningly. That New York apartment, the color schemes, the lighting style—

That's Pato Guzman. It was the first movie to show SoHo. If there is a movie that showed it before mine, it might have been a very low budget film I don't know about. But Hollywood was not shooting there. Another Mazursky mistake is that I could have bought SoHo. For about half a million bucks I could have bought three buildings that would now be worth thirty million dollars. But I was

---

31   Iron Eyes Cody was the quintessential American Indian in countless movies and TV shows. In 1996 a New Orleans newspaper exposed him as Espera DeCorti, an Italian. He died in 1999 at age 92.

too busy looking at locations and wasn't interested in real estate. The apartment was very difficult to shoot in—way up high with all those windows. We found someone who was in some group run by a Chilean friend of Pato's wife and we had to get permission from the building, which we got. But then the building was very angry with us. I shot in the lobby, I shot in front of the building, I shot upstairs, all the wires and this and that. We got away with it, but it was a nightmare. In order to light it, we had to put window washers' scaffolding to get light in.

There's a shot of the actors inside where you see it's night outside. It's a practical shot, but I thought it was a cyclorama at first.

No, that's all Arthur Ornitz. And Pato, who understood what you could do. And also, by the way, quick. That movie took forty days, all those locations. Incredible.

You can feel the atmosphere of New York.

There are helicopter shots, there's hand held shots, there's jogging shots, there's Chinatown, there's the West Side Highway. All over New York city. There are seasonal changes in this movie. We scouted certain things, but we had forgotten that New York has seasons, and by the time we got to shoot in April and May, buds were coming out when we were supposed to be doing winter scenes. So we had to clip the buds and put our own trees in the foreground and put snow on them. We had to do tricks. Then we had Alan Bates and Jill walking near NYU. Bates was a great choice, one of my favorite people. I offered the part first to Anthony Hopkins (dry laugh) when he was not yet a big star. His agent turned it down saying it's too small, he doesn't come into the film until page 75. And I said, "But he dominates the next 40 pages. It's a star turn. Are you crazy?" I then went to Alan Arkin, who happened to be in the building, in some office, not romantic but I figured maybe I'll go against type, instead of making him romantic, I'll make him this real Jewish artist. Arkin was sort of noncommittal and sort of said in so many words, "I don't play these parts so good where I take my shirt off." Something like that. I respect him. So he didn't do it. So I said the hell with it, I'm going for a great actor who's a gorgeous hunk in some way and I contacted Alan Bates, who read it and said, on the phone, "But he's a Jewish guy from New York." And I said, "No he's not, Alan. He's a British Jew and I will make it clear in the script, which I'll send you in two days with a tiny rewrite. You can have the accent and everything. And you've been living in New York for nine years and I'll find you a list right now of ten artists who are from England who live in New York." And then he said, "Look, I really want to do it, but my father is dying right here in England and I'm just terribly afraid to commit to something in New York." I said, "Let me come to London to meet you and talk about the problem and see what we can do." So I come to London and I meet him over breakfast. We like each other. I said, "I really want to make this movie. Here's the best I can do: you're in New York, you get a call your father's taken a turn for the worst, you have seven days off. It's my problem what I shoot. It's a small gamble on my part. It could be in the middle of the biggest scene in the movie, I guarantee it." So he did it. No nonsense, the Brits. He just showed up and did it. He came for rehearsals, God I'm fond of him. When the movie was over, his father died.

The film is in pastels until we meet Bates, and he's using these bold colors in his paintings; of course, he's bringing color into her life.

He was taught how to paint by Paul Jenkins. The painter whose paintings I use taught Alan how to throw the paint with the ivory knife. And then when the movie was over, Alan asked Paul Jenkins if he could keep the painting that he had made, and Paul refused because he felt—he didn't say it, but this is what he meant—that if people think anybody can do it, it reduced the value of his work. But Paul gave Alan one of his; a very valuable one. I have a great Jenkins now in my home, too, a beautiful one. By the way, all the scenes in the loft were Paul Jenkins' loft.

You use therapists in a lot of your films. Is there a utilitarian purpose for that?

What do you mean "utilitarian"?

For exposition.

One of the things about my characters in most of the movies I've made, certainly from 1970 to 1990, those 20 years, and even later (not *Moon Over Parador* or *Moscow on the Hudson*) is that they're middle, upper-middle class people, for the most part, who were, in those days, extremely into therapy. The kind of therapy changes over the years, but the search for answers [continues], including far eastern and near-eastern philosophies, most of which have profound truths in them, but are also ridiculous, in that people think that, by putting on a robe and going to an ashram, they're gong to pick up wisdom. You can't do it unless you live that life. I'm gonna get killed for this, but there I am saying it. However, therapy was part and parcel of the lives of everybody I knew personally and still know, although now it's less in fashion. People now go to psychologists; at the time that I was starting, they were going to analysis three times a week, lying down on the couch.

The psychiatrist scenes in An Unmarried Woman ***have a very different feel, very real, and therefore sort of threatening.***

The closest thing to improvisation in any of my movies is probably the psychologist, Penelope Russianoff, who I told, "when you do the scenes with Jill Clayburgh, if something happens that takes you off on any tangent, do it." And I told Jill, "the script is written, but if she hits you with something, you've got to go with it." Jill was magnificent. She started to fall apart and she said, "I don't understand why this is happening to me." And Penelope said, "You're discombobulated." Well, Jill looked up at her with a look you couldn't write. Discombobulated? Some of the best scenes might come out of something that's absolutely unplanned, that you never come up with in a step outline.

So they had a very, very firm grasp of character.

We shot them about a month into the picture. Jill had a fairly firm grasp of her character. Penelope was a little nervous, but I shot it in her apartment and I did it the way she worked. She worked with the person on the floor on pillows, which is already hilarious, but it's real. Jill started to cry. She lost it. I had two cameras and I had to shoot it a couple times, but I got almost all of it in one take. Then I did a second scene, and when the studio tested the movie they asked me to cut one of the two scenes out. It felt long to them. And I cut the scene out for myself and ran the picture for myself and the editor, Stuart Pappé, and it didn't work. The information we missed was profoundly important, so I put it back. And, of course, the movie was a smash hit of the highest order, so you don't know. But to give the studio credit, they never fought me.

Men in our society are supposed to be strong. In many of your films it's the women who are strong.

Middle class men in America tend not to be as strong as women, I agree. Bob and Ted and Blume and Martin.

It was important that you created Saul's character as the product of a divorce, too, but it was his wife who left him. Had he left his wife it would have made him an unfavorable character.

That helped, I think.

The film's style is different from your other movies. One almost feels voyeuristic watching intimate scenes between these people.

Do you know the scene in one of the bedrooms with the four women, when Kelley Bishop (Elaine) breaks down and all the women comfort her? The lab ruined the scene. It was destroyed; a guy fell asleep. I had close to a nervous breakdown. You get insurance—

— but you still had to redo it—

— and it was better! There was no risk now. It was better. By luck. I'm good at that; I'm good at capturing the intimacy.

Have there been times when Paul Mazursky, the writer, has written Paul Mazursky, the director, into a corner?

I've had scenes that were not working, and it's always for one of two reasons: either the scene doesn't work in the first place and you didn't know it till you got on the damn floor, or an actor can't cut it. In *An Unmarried Woman* there was an actress, who is not [now] in the picture, just couldn't do it. She read great, and I shot it, but it didn't work and I ended up cutting that scene out of the movie. I should have re-cast it and shot it another day. [In the story] Michael Green (Michael Murphy), the husband, leaves his wife for this other woman whom he met at Bloomingdale's. I have a scene later in the movie where the woman from Bloomingdale's goes to the art gallery for help from Jill Clayburgh. She's living with him now and he's all fucked up and she goes to Jill for advice! It's a wonderful scene but it just didn't work.

Why?

It just didn't. I don't know to this day whether it was the actress or the scene.

IT'S NOT A REMAKE OF JULES AND JIM!

Nat Segaloff: *With the huge success of* An Unmarried Woman, *you launched into* Willie & Phil[32], *a much more elegiac film which traces the landscape of a profoundly changing America by looking at the lives and friendship of three close friends.*

Paul Mazursky: I got rapped—oh, gosh, I got rapped—they thought I was daring to remake *Jules and Jim*. I wasn't trying to remake *Jules and Jim*. I'm not a moron! At the end of *Jules and Jim* Catherine (Jeanne Moreau) drives off a bridge! I was trying to say that in today's times—which was in 1977—we'd reached the point where it's not out of the question that two guys in love with the same gal could share her, take turns, and still be best friends. I've heard stories like this, and maybe you have too; they're not commonplace, but it happens. I thought it might be clever to have them be movie buffs and to have them meet at a screening of *Jules and Jim*, which I begin the picture with, and is one of my favorite movies.

Here, as in a number of your films, the characters tend to have middle or upper-middle class ennui *where, to the audience, things are going great, but to them, something's happening that makes them doubt their existence.*

---

32 Unsettled Willie (Michael Ontkean), wired Phil (Ray Sharkey), and earthy, ethereal Jeanette (Margot Kidder) pass through the 70s and 80s exploring life, relationships, commitment (and lack thereof), finally settling on the thing they least expected: normalcy.

I don't like to use the word *ennui*. *Willie & Phil*, these two guys—you can call it *ennui*—but, really, it's that they're both crazy about the same gal, and they love each other very much. *Ennui*, to me, means more: "I have everything and I don't feel good." A good psychiatrist will tell you that the hardest thing to deal with is *ennui*. It's much easier to deal with nervous breakdowns, real problems, people who have suffered great loss, a divorce, a death, cancer. *Ennui* is impossible to deal with. You might as well say, "Take an aspirin." That's why Prozac is so big.

Willie & Phil struck me emotionally and, when it came out, of course, it was about my people and my generation.

It's one of Steven Spielberg's favorites. He saw the movie, wrote me a letter saying, "How do you make these kind of movies, these relationships?" I said, "How do you make these kind of movies where guys are on a boat chasing a giant shark?" I said, "I wouldn't know how to do that. You're a genius. You could do what I'm doing and, if I can sound pretentious, Steven, you've got to start digging into your own life." That was the end of it. But he really liked it.

Well, he should. It's one of those films that's not nostalgia, but it is nostalgic, and by the end of it you feel a yearning for its beginning.

I would like to take a look at it again. It's been a long time. The movie was shot probably seven weeks or so in New York and about three weeks in California, and because of the split, the cinematographers union refused to let Arthur Ornitz photograph it because he didn't have a California union card. It was a terrible blow to Arthur, who had done *An Unmarried Woman* and *Next Stop, Greenwich Village*. Arthur was a brilliant cinematographer who had a history of not being liked by certain people. His father was Samuel Ornitz, who was blacklisted.[33] I fought for Arthur and

---

33 Ornitz was one of the Hollywood Ten cited for Contempt of Congress for refusing to discuss their political affiliations with the House Un-American Activities Committee in 1947, leading to the Hollywood Blacklist.

I lost. They said to get someone who has a card in both unions. I said to show me the list, and I see Sven Nykvist, Ingmar Bergman's brilliant cinematographer. I send him the script, and he likes it, and we do it. It broke Arthur's heart. Sven and I became great pals, and that was a great experience, because, to work with Bergman's guy meant a lot of wonderful things.

What is it he does? Does he use chimera for lighting? Frame differently?

Sven doesn't have much patience with many takes, but once you decide on the set up you're going to make, he lights very quickly, and he seems to have a brilliant and uncanny ability to come up with the right light for the scene that gives it an emotional texture that, as smart as you think you are as a director, and as visual as you think you are, Sven has something going in there that gives it a texture that takes you in emotionally. He knows how to do it and he's quick.

Were there gels? Diffusion?

Yeah, we fought about diffusion. I don't like diffusion.

On the lights or the lens?

On the lens. We had a tiny bit of diffusion because he wanted to try something and I didn't want it. He begged me and showed me some tests and finally I said, "Do the tiniest bit." Diffusion makes it look softer, often used for older women to make them look better, and we didn't need that. That's one great memory. And, of course, we had a sequence in the character of Willie, who is on a search, as many people were in the sixties, for the truth. He goes off to India to find the answer. With the studios in those days, the directors were so wonderfully powerful—I didn't know it, we just took it for granted—that when I casually said, "I can't shoot this stuff in India on the back lot," they said, "Work out a budget." It was 100 Gs. I took Sven, Tony Ray[34] the co-producer, a make up and a hair person, and an assistant cameraman and one other assistant and we went to India. We went to Darjeeling, Calcutta, New Delhi, and Varanarsi on the Ganges—what a great time—to shoot this little thing that ended up maybe three minutes. I went into Buddhist temples. Those memories last forever. And then when the movie came out—! I knew going in that I was taking a risk where two guys meet at a screening in a theatre in New York of *Jules and Jim*, that [the critics] were all gonna say, "You're trying to remake *Jules and Jim*." Well, of course, it was *inspired* by *Jules and Jim* but it had nothing to do with *Jules and Jim* except for one fact: it's two guys and a girl.

Whose name is "Jeanette" and not "Jeanne."

Right, but everything is completely different. What I was exploring was the fact that we had been given permission in my scheme of things—coming from *Bob & Carol & Ted & Alice* where the real bourgeois couples were slightly ready to experiment with "Shall we switch?" "Are we sexually free yet?" and were still square, to *Blume in Love* where a guy cheats on his wife once and is kicked out, but by God things have changed because he rapes his ex-wife and she gets pregnant and she takes him back at the end. So life was changing. And by the 70s when I made *Willie & Phil* I was saying to saying to myself, "I think it's possible now for two guys to be in love with the same girl and they don't hate each other. They're friends. They all love each other." That's what the movie was about: trying to explore those friendships. Well, the movie had its fans; it did okay. It also had its detractors. You never know. When a movie like that came out like that in those days, if they don't think it's gonna make it, they release it on an art house level and it plays for maybe a month or six weeks, and then they do their best to pump it out in Europe. And that's what happened.

It's a terrifically avant-garde film in which the characters seemed like an extension of the Elmo character from Blume in Love in

---

34 Tony Ray was the son of celebrated director Nicholas Ray.

that they take things as they come and they react to them without an agenda.

The character that Michael Ontkean played—the one who was trying to be hip—is on his way to becoming an Elmo by going to India and searching for the answer and sitting there with the gurus. He's on his way to "Aw, nothin' to it," which was Elmo's line. Paul Mazursky never found that. I was on the search, but I would have never gone to India if not for the movie, and I never had a guru, even though I still read books and dabble in Buddhism and I love the ideas. But I'm not a meditator. My meditations, I think I've done them when I wake up, and it's four and a half minutes. But I like the ideas.

There's much more use of voice-over in the final cut of Willie & Phil *than is indicated in the script. Sometimes they provide transition between sequences, and other times they bridge a truncated sequence with a description.*

You know, we all steal from other movies. You'd be crazy not to. It's the same as painters. You can't meet a good painter who won't tell, you he's inspired by Velasquez or Goya even though they're painting a weird canvas with three lines on it. You're influenced. One of the things that influenced—now that I've finished telling you that I wasn't trying to make *Jules and Jim*—was that Truffaut had this brilliant instinct for moving a film along cinematically without pretense in the matter of (snaps fingers) a second by saying, "We went to Paris." Suddenly the screen flips, dissolves, wipes, a voice has said this to you, and you're in Paris. There's no long establishing shots, he just moves it. Voice-overs are like a good drug.

They can also make a film novelistic.

They can work brilliantly or they can tear you down. I just read a script that has so many voice-overs that I had trouble reading it. It may be possible, as I said to the person I spoke to about it, that when you make the movie you'll find you don't need them all. But usually they're put in there to give information that the author of the script has no other way to give.

They're usually a liability. People say, when there are voice-overs, that the director has done something wrong with the scene.

When you say "people" you don't mean the audience, 'cause the audience doesn't think of that. It's not that they're stupid, but just entertain them, involve them, and you're fine. There are no rules. You can use voice-overs.

There are voice-overs that are one of the characters, which impart a different feeling from one that is an objective voice-over—

—that's true—

—there are voice-overs that are judgmental and some that are not judgmental, some that work in counterpoint, some that merely narrate—

The voice-over in *Willie & Phil* is mine. It was an open call to the critics to say, "Boy, he must be nervous that we don't get his movie" or something like that. Truffaut used that third voice; it's not the voice of any of his characters. One of the great voice-overs was by Billy Wilder in *Sunset Boulevard* where the dead guy, whom we see floating in the pool, tells the story. It was a brilliant device and it works.

At what point did you add more voice-over?

I was determined to keep it throughout from the beginning, but I don't remember, frankly, whether I added or subtracted. My tendency is usually to take out. I knew I needed the voice-over. The film plays around with time a lot. It moves over a period of at least a decade. There's a child, and the child's growth helps you, the journey to India, the trip to California. The passage of time is sometimes clearly evident but I felt it needed a little help so I did some voice-overs.

Margot Kidder, who plays Jeanette, has had a very unusual, even tragic, career.

When I was casting the part I read every young actress in New York and LA. I could have had Meryl Streep. Meryl wanted to have casting okay of the two guys, and I told my agent, who was also her agent, no actress is going to tell me who I am going to use in a movie. So I passed. Mandy Patinkin played Willie and he was pretty good, but I went another way. I wanted Ray Sharkey. I met Glenn Close and this one and that one, and Margot came along and was like—I didn't know her that well—she was not a hippie but she was a free spirit. She was like Jeanette. One of the guys who read for the part of Willie was John Heard, the American actor, very talented, and he's really rich in irony. I cast him in the part and he fell in love with Margot at the reading, and before I knew it they were an item. I hadn't yet started the movie. He got so crazed with Margot that he called me one day and said, "I don't want to see her involved with another actor in this movie. I can't do it." I was very angry. Margot begged me to keep him but I couldn't. We got along well and she was no trouble. I like her very much. Later on, these things that happened with her, I can't explain and I have no idea. She's smart. You know, she was married to Tom McGuane, the novelist. He's the father of her child. She's a dandy lady. I wish her well.[35]

In the course of the story, they come back from a movie theatre after doing acid and there's a lot more dialogue on the screen than there is for that same scene in the script. At what point did you and the actors decide that you needed more dialogue to make the scene play?

---

[35] In 1997 Margot Kidder was discovered living as a bag lady in Los Angeles. She was given help for a psychological condition and moved to Montana where died of a drug overdose on May 13, 2018.

They were going through a thing where there might not have been enough words there. Less is more for me. I don't really think you need any words sometimes. If they need a line, sure, since I'm the author or co-author of all these movies, I would always [give them a line], but after they do it a few times they very often didn't need the line. They give the actor time to feel comfortable. The actor is the one who has to do it. The actor is your collaborator, and if the actor's uncomfortable, if the actress is really not comfortable, you get a certain kind of acting that, when I see it, I know right away that they're not comfortable. They're doing what I call controlled pushing. They're very good at it, but I can see it. I can smell it.

Some of the scenes in Willie & Phil—and I also noticed it in Harry & Tonto and some others—you cut away from the scene before it ends in the script. The blackout moment comes before the place where you wrote for it to come. When do you make those decisions?

When I look at the full assembly. Sometimes I would start one page in. My theory is, Let them act three pages, you knowing that you might only need two. Not that you will make interior cuts to make it shorter, though I've done that, too, but maybe they need six or eight lines to warm up, but it's all bullshit.
"Where you been?"
"I've been out to the thing."
"You were supposed to come here at four o'clock."
"It's only four thirty."
"Jesus Christ."
And the next line is, "So what's happening, is he gonna do it?" And I start the scene with that.

There's a large chunk cut at the end of Willie & Phil—pages 103 to 112—where they're discussing Buñuel's film, where Willie calls Jeanette a sphinx, where Phil talks about his salami nightmare, and then they all go to Phil's therapist.

All cut. I played the therapist. I felt you didn't need it. When I saw the movie I felt it began to drag and the easiest thing for me to cut was myself. I was brutal. In retrospect, a couple years later I looked at the scene again, and I kinda liked it, and I was ambivalent.

Finally, the narrator says, "And in the end they grew up and were normal." So that by the time Willie and Phil come out of the second screening of Jules and Jim, they didn't get it. They haven't changed. Yet Jeanette and the audience have profoundly changed.

The stuff that happened to them hadn't made them better, hadn't made them worse, hadn't made them hipper. They'd just been on this journey that a lot of people were on in that period, and real life took over. As you get older you have to go about the business of making a living. Without saying it. They'd had these great times which they'll always remember.

As they leave the revival theatre they pass people lining up for a midnight screening of The Rocky Horror Picture Show.

Those are the new ones. They go at night to act out the parts in front of the screen. It's a hip ending. Whether the masses caught it, I don't know. I always liked the movie a lot and I thought that the editor, Don Cameron, did a wonderful job, that it had wonderful rhythms. The music was by a great French composer, Claude Bolling. The way I got him was that during the course of making every movie I've ever made, I almost always find what I call "the music" for that movie, and it's music I use to inspire me while I'm writing the script and while I'm thinking about the shots and planning it. I don't always intend to use it. In *Moscow on the Hudson* I kept playing Ben Webster on the sax over and over again, plus some Russian circus music I found. I'd play it in the office while I was writing. For this movie I decided I'd call Claude Bolling and I'd get him here to America, and show him the movie. He loved it and said, "I'll do it." I used some of what I'd heard. He wrote more music. He's a great jazz pianist. Great. That score gave it a kind of lyrical French feeling. In retrospect, maybe I should have given it a more American feeling because the movie, even though they had gotten their ideas from *Jules and Jim*, a deliberate friendship: hello, I'm Willie, hello, I'm Phil. It's only in New York. I don't know if that could happen here in L.A. People here go to the movies at malls. The malls are not conducive to friendships.

Julie Bovasso's scene, where she slaps her son, Ray Sharkey, for living in sin, is stunning. I felt that slap.

She's great. She really hit him. Ray was shocked. Julie Bovasso and the man who played her husband, Louis Guss—I wanted to make an Italian family that had absolutely every attribute of [Willie's] Jewish family. I had many Italian friends who always told me, when I would tell all those stories about my mother, "Paul, come to my house," and, sure enough, the Italian mother would go, "Eat! Eat! Did I make all this food for nothing?" and they would be cleaning up under my feet. My mother used to clean while you were eating. On the table, too, wiping up under your dish as you finish the first course. My mother had an anger that Julie's the queen of. Julie was great. She's a brilliant actress and a great coach. Those are memorable things to me.

At the end, Jeanette is working on a documentary called Moscow on the Hudson.

I was thinking about doing it and I had her go off with the Russian guy.

THREE OF A KIND

Nat Segaloff: Your next three films have a unity: Tempest, Moscow on the Hudson *and* Down and Out in Beverly Hills. *All were written by you and Leon Capetanos, photographed by Don McAlpine, and designed by Pato Guzman. They work in different ways, but each shows a filmmaker at the height of his powers. How did you get together with Leon Capetanos?*

Paul Mazursky: My agent, Jeff Berg, said to me one day, "I've got a script you ought to read by a guy named Leon Capetanos. It's called *White on White*." It was set in post-World War I in Paris, a clever, erudite relationship, not *Jules and Jim*, but there was something good about the writing. I really liked it, but I decided not to make it and, instead, wanted to meet the guy who wrote it. I met with him and really liked him, and some time went by and I said, "I've been fooling around with an idea of trying to make a movie out of *The Tempest*." I don't remember when Leon came aboard during the time I was thinking about it, because I had first talked about making it into a musical, and I'd met Mick Jagger to play Ariel. I was gonna do it like a traveling group of actors in the Mediterranean in their own little boat and they go from island to island and they're rehearsing *Tempest* on the boat when a storm comes, and they go into the play. They talk like actors at the beginning—"you got any more pancake?"—and they get washed ashore and then I go into the play. I was going to do it in the language of Shakespeare. But I couldn't figure it out. Then I struck upon another idea which started to ring true for me: the main character, Prospero, is in the midst of a bad divorce and he's got his daughter with him, and they get to the island. I didn't know quite how to do it. I had them coming from the Cannes Film Festival where he had a movie. Then I decided, "Don't make him in the movie business, get away from show business." I asked myself, "In what profession or art does one dream or fantasize enough that you would be as crazy as I think Prospero is?" I decided it was architecture. I'd heard about a guy named Solari who was working in the southwest, and I went to see him. He's been building a city for 25 years. He's possessed. He sells bells to make money for the place, and architectural students come to visit him, and I saw it. It's like a beehive complex with everything: theatres, rooms, it'll never be finished. The Arcoleum, some name like that. He's a very intense little guy, reminded me of Kazan. I asked him, "Do you know *Tempest*?" He said, "I know the play." I told him what I was doing and I asked him if he thought an architect could be capable of those fantasies. He said, "This one is." I knew I was on the right track.

Then Leon and I spent a lot of time discussing it. Leon wrote a draft, and I worked on the draft, and we just kept on going back and forth with it until finally it evolved, and when I got John Cassavetes I made everything Greek, because Cassavetes is Greek. I made it a Greek island[36]. When I was looking for locations I started in Hawaii and Baja, California and Catalina. None of them seemed right. And I knew that the actual storm in Shakespeare is in the Bermudas, interestingly enough. There's a lot of research you can do on *Tempest*, a lot of books, great drawings. I found a great book of French drawings that that person's vision of what Shakespeare wrote with great paintings, and I used those. I gave them to Pato Guzman, and the costumer, Albert Wolsky, and Don McAlpine, and they inspired us a lot in the framing of shots and how things looked.

---

36 Embittered architect Philip Demetrios (John Cassavetes) leaves his wife (Gena Rowlands) because of her affair with businessman Vittorio Gassman. He and their daughter (Molly Ringwald) flee to a Greek island inhabited by goats and their herder Kalibanos (Raul Julia). They are joined by American expatriate Susan Sarandon. When Gassman and his sycophants show up on a yacht, Cassavetes magically conjures a storm that tosses everyone together.

When Leon and I finally had a good draft, we gave it to Alan Ladd, Jr. Fox had paid for the draft, but by the time the draft was finished, the Ladd group had left Fox. I think it was because Laddie had made a fortune for them with *Star Wars* and they gave him a very small bonus, a raise, and he was very upset and he went out and formed his own company [the Ladd Company, releasing through Warner Bros.]. I quickly brought the project to him and they were afraid to do it as their first picture. So I went to Frank Price [at Columbia] thinking that I've got another one of these projects that no one's gonna wanna do. Well, he called me the next day and said, "I want to do it."

When you write with Leon, does one have a yellow pad, does the other type, do you do a beat sheet, what?

We just talk a lot and then, one way or the other, I will type out a lot of scenes, a step outline, and then Leon will take it over, We have worked a little differently on some scripts. Some scripts we've worked on, he always does the writing by himself and then I take it and do the writing by myself. Some more than others. In the case of *Tempest* he wrote a version, I took it and I went to Palm Springs myself, and did a lot of work on it. In the case of *Moscow on the Hudson*, he wrote a version, and the biggest change I made was to change the girl from an American to an Italian. In the case of the thing I just did with Leon, *Iron Eyes Cody*, he wrote the whole script, but we talked for months, we did research for months, we went to places, we met people together. That's how we did it. It's what a producer does, or a good director. Leon's a wonderful writer. When we did *Moon Over Parador*, I went on a scouting trip with Pato Guzman and took Leon with me so he could see what I was looking for while we were writing the script. In those days, one was somehow able to get money for a scout and take an extra person. Right now I'm thinking about doing something for Showtime and they don't even pay for a scout in Vancouver, and I can't make a decision till I've scouted, and they won't pay for three days; they're very cautions about spending ten dollars. So they've not only taken the pleasure out of it all, they've made it a little crazy because, as you know, preparation and scouting and research are what make things richer. In the case of *Tempest*, I had people scouting all over. I finally met Michael Cacoyanis [director of *Zorba the Greek*, among other films] at a party at the French embassy in LA—we didn't really *know* each other but we knew *of* each other—and he asked me what I was doing.

I said, "Right now I'm in a lot of trouble. I think I have a 'go' movie but I don't know where to shoot it. I can't find this thing that's in my head."

"What's in your head?" he said.

I said, "Well..," and I sort of described it.

"Oh," he said, "you mean stone villages with towers and turrets."

I said, "Yes."

He said, "Go to the Mani."

"The Mani?"

"The Peloponnesus. It's there. Go here, go there, you find plenty of it." I went, and he was right.

At what point do you articulate characters and start tracking them through the story?

At the beginning. When you start, you talk about what kind of guy he is, what's his relationship with his wife, what's his relationship with his daughter. You talk about that as much as you can before you've written. As a writer, you know that, in some cases, you can have a vague idea but it's not three-dimensional until you start to write—and then it only becomes really three-dimensional if, when you're writing, [you discover that] it's only one-dimensional [because] you've done something wrong. Now you've got to figure out precisely, "What am I gonna do here?" So you add stuff onto the character's life—his baggage, her baggage—you don't necessarily even write about it, you just know about it.

I never did this, but I always thought it: you're doing a movie about a guy who has to move quick in life. And you realize there's something missing. Well, you break his leg. Now he's got to operate with a broken leg for most of the movie, this guy who moves like a bullet through life. But now he's got a problem, and it makes it a little more interesting.

We talk about character, which comes a lot from my training as an actor where, as an actor, I would try to create a background for the character. You take what's given you by the playwright or the movie writer and you fill it in. Some actors don't bother with any of the filling-in, but having been trained in the "method"—which I don't worship, but I was trained that way and I believe in it a lot—it sometimes helps. You feel comfortable so that you know, if there's a desk in the movie, you know where you bought it. I got this desk at an antique sale on Melrose Avenue three years ago and I re-stained it. And then you know that so that when you're acting the part and you put your hand on the desk [Mazursky caresses his desktop] you know it's the desk you re-stained. That sort of thing. Well, in writing you can't share everything with a partner, but if you trust each other you let that partner go as far as he can. I did the same thing with Josh Greenfeld in *Harry & Tonto*. He would write, I would write more, and we'd take each other's and fool around with it. Sometimes it works very well, and sometimes you strike out. Sometimes the writer who's your partner who does the draft goes off into places you don't really want, and you have to get it back on track. Collaboration is a process.

In Tempest, **there's a certain feeling of danger watching Cassavetes act. Did you feel that working with him?**

Never having worked with him, the reputation that preceded him was of this improviser who never did it the same way twice, *et cetera*. None of it's true. He did it the same, but not *exactly* the same, only it was the same intentions. He had surprises, which gave him a kind of danger. If I had to generalize, it was a very pleasant experience. There were times he'd want to do something and he'd say to me, "You know, I want to get something in here about baseball. This guy's not gonna be on the island and not know. He's got to be..." So I said, okay, put something in there, and he wrote, "DiMaggio, he hit 56 straight..." out of nowhere he's talking about baseball to Raul Julia, and it worked. Other times, he'd be talking about electrical storms and I didn't know what he was talking about and neither did Susan Sarandon. Leon wasn't there; I was the only one there. Oddly enough, Leon's family was from the area where I shot, in the mountains, near a town called Githeon. "Capetanos" means "captain." Yeah, there's a certain danger with John, which I think was real good for this part.

His scenes with Gena in the New York apartment. First, you were using production sound, which is very rare—

— Yeah—

I felt ashamed to be watching it, it was so real.

It was great. "I hate that fucking cat, I hate this place. . ." A few of those he added. I always gave him permission, so to speak, to not worry about the lines, but John Cassavetes stayed 90 percent on the lines, and Gena 100. Gena's a great actress. A parentheses in the movie: in the scene where he comes home drunk, that great party scene [in which Paul and Betsy Mazursky portray guests], it's one of my favorite scenes in any movie I've done because it has a reality to it you don't often see about the uncomfortableness of someone's husband being drunk and the party getting weird and the way people are. Betsy had one line, which is, "Come on, let's go home," and John makes me dance with him. The dancing was improvised.

You didn't know it was going to happen before that take?

No. He did it and I went with it. That was pretty funny, I must say. But Betsy says her line and we finished the take—the scene was a big argument—and John says, in front of everybody, and with Gena right there, "I just had the privilege of working with the best actress I've ever worked with in my life." I think he's talking about Gena. Instead, he says, "Betsy, you're fantastic." She's not an actress. So we all giggle and laugh. Now he won't let it go. Every day you show up on the set and he [applauds], "How's the greatest actress I've ever worked with?" He gives her a party in Rome for her birthday. There were fifty, a hundred people there. "I want to salute the greatest actress I've ever worked with, bar none!" Is he doing this to tease Gena? He's not, because Gena doesn't care; she's secure. Well, all this is hilarious and we have a great time and the movie's over and we come back to LA. About two or three weeks pass and I get a phone call and it's John, who says, "Is Betsy there?"

I said, "Yeah."

"Lemme talk to her."

"It's for you."

So I hear her with Cassavetes on the phone, "Where? In the Valley? The lead? You want me? Oh, no, I couldn't go to the Valley." He wants her to come to a reading on Sunday with Dustin Hoffman and Peter Falk and play the lead woman because she's the greatest actress he ever worked with. She turned him down.

You indicate in your book that some of the head games that Cassavetes played with Gena were to feed his character's relationship with her character.

That's all true. He told Gena that he was going to sacrifice the goat [in the film] for real and kill the goat, and she told me she's not doing the scene. So they were very pissed off at each other—or it looked like the were—and they took it out on me. I was, at first, thinking it was a joke, but then as we got closer to shooting, she was saying, "I'm not gonna do it."

He says, "I'm killing the goat."

I said, "John, you're not killing any goat. We get an animal skin, we cut away, we cut back…"

We had a scene in a restaurant—I wrote about it in the book—where she went to the bathroom and never came back. I hardly slept. The next day I see them walking onto the set with their arms around each other. They had taken it as far as they could take it.

At what point did you and Leon decide to do the broad strokes of the Tempest *story in discontinuous time?*

I don't remember exactly, but it evolved as we wrote the script. I fooled around with time a couple of times; I did it with *Blume in Love* and I certainly did it in *Tempest* where you're going from them having an argument in a taxicab and then there you are in Greece, or vice-versa. We just used these very visual cuts to take us. It was the first time I worked with [cinematographer] Don McAlpine. Maybe I should tell you that story.

Tempest was originally supposed to be photographed by Sven Nykvist. Then Sven called me and said that he'd gotten a call from Bergman. "Paul, he is going to make a film called 'Fanny, Alexander' or something and I have to do it." I said, "I quite understand, Sven, go do it." I then called Pepino [Giuseppe] Rotunno, Fellini's guy, and he said he'd do it. Then a few days later Rotunno called and said, "I've got bad news. Fellini's going to make something called *Amarcord*." So now I've struck out twice. That week I went to the movies and saw *Breaker Morant*. Great outdoor visuals. Australian, Bruce Beresford, Don McAlpine. So I got hold of [producer-actor-director] Tony Bill who knew Bruce and I said, "Ask Bruce what about this McAlpine guy?" Tony called back and said, "Bruce told me to tell you he's great, he's fast, he's wonderful and here's his number." So I call McAlpine and I had a very hard time understanding him because he had a very thick—at that time—Australian accent. I mean *thick*: "Awryte mate, I'd do loyke tayve it, do dat." ?? I said, "Look, I'll send you the script, read it and call me." So he reads it and calls me and it's a good conversation. He's clearly a bright man. I said, "Look, I don't feel like flying to Australia. I've now seen three movies you've made. Let's do it. I'll meet you in Greece." I knocked on his door in Athens and there's a little guy with a beard and a twinkle in his eye. I really have trouble understanding him, and I'm good with accents. I said, "Mate. Could. You. Talk. A. Little. Slower?" We got along magnificently and made four pictures together and he's now got this terrific relationship with Baz Luhrmann. He did *Moulin Rouge, Strictly Ballroom, Romeo and Juliet* and *Hunt for Red October*. He's great and he's smart and he's fast. I like him very much. If people understood how much he contributed, he would get an Oscar® or at least a nomination.

Shakespeare begins with a tempest. You end with a tempest.

I got punished by the critics for calling it *Tempest*. I never called it *THE Tempest*, I called it *Tempest*. A lot of critics said, "Who the hell is he to dare to make a movie of Shakespeare's last play? He's not a Shakespearean, he's not this, he's not that. . ." It's so offensive, those moronic reviews. First of all, you can dare to do anything you want to do. Secondly, I was clearly using it as a framework, but it's *completely* different. It's Americanized, its use of the storm and magic, it's a very personal and strange way to do it, not like Shakespeare's. I did one thing that I thought was Shakespearean but nobody notices it: out of nowhere I had songs. I gave Raul Julia the famous goat dance to *New York, New York*[37]. I had Susan and Molly do a song. Shakespeare would do songs now and then.

I was in *Fear and Desire*, Stanley Kubrick's first film, and I played the role of Sidney, a crazed G.I. who ends up raping a girl against a tree. During the time that I have my nervous breakdown in the movie, I sing, from *The Tempest*, "Full fathom five thy father lies/ his bones are coral made/those are pearls that were his eyes/ nothing of him that doth fade. . ." I was 21 years old; all these years later I tied it back into my life. Nobody else knows that. But if I had not called it *Tempest* and called it *The Crazy Architect*, maybe they would have been kinder. But, boy, were they stupid. I've gotten good reviews and bad reviews and mediocre reviews and vague reviews. I've gotten rave reviews. What I don't like is when they write a review of a movie I didn't make.

What works so well, I think, is that where Shakespeare uses the storm to begin his play, you use the storm to resolve yours. I've never understood why Prospero would want to conjure the storm, since he loses because of it.

---

37 The anthem to the Apple by John Kander and Fred Ebb.

When we wrote the script it became clear, as we were fooling around, that the storm would be the climax of his conflicts. That was one of the big changes we made. It's actually, on a very simple level, about a man who has stopped paying attention to his wife [and she] goes off and has an affair. It's a very powerful thing. When he gets hold of the daughter who can't stand the fact that her mother has had this affair, they run off together. Ariel, in the play, is a sprite, almost magical; Susan [Sarandon] was anything but that. Susan was great, but we made her a zaftig, funny, funky, open gal. During the course of this thing, his craziness takes him into building a theatre. Then when he sees [his wife, her lover, and their entourage] in the water, is the storm a real storm? Did he make the storm? Is it a magical storm? He thinks he made it. In any case, it's a way to resolve this thing that's been burning in his brain for a year.

The tango sequence near the end of the film both describes and resolves the characters' complex relationships.

That was shot in studio. All of the stuff in the daytime on the island was shot on the island. The house, the outside, in the beginning taking the shower, all of that is clearly a real island. And it wasn't an island, it was a cove an hour's drive from Githeon. But Pato built the house itself at Cinecittà so we could control the moves. It's impossible to move cameras that way—

— without balancing on a rock ledge—

— it's impossible. We also used the tank at Cinecittà for the storm. The storm is a combination of stuff done in the tank, computer-generated shots—even then—and stuff shot at another location nearby in the Mani where they go out swimming to save her. That was one of the only days of this entire summer when the water was rough, which was good. I had two lifeguards and Cassavetes and Gena and Vittorio Gassman and Susan Sarandon and the tall model were out there swimming. I was scared to death. I might have done something risky but they all said they'd do it. It was rough. And all the twilight stuff, magic hour, when they come up on the shore and they're all safe? That was all done in one night. I prepped for it all day, laid the track, rehearsed the scene, and by 3 o'clock we had it rehearsed. Then we took a rest. Don McAlpine was always prompt and would say, "At thirteen minutes after five the sun will be over there, we will be over there, and we can make our first shot. It won't be the one we're gonna use, but it will be a good rehearsal. At 5:45 we'll be in a position to do the second shot." We had three cracks at it and we did it.

When were the curtain calls done? It didn't look like an interior.

That was the real cove. And that curtain call is one of my favorite things. But, see, I had the freedom then. It doesn't break my heart, but it does make me yearn for the good old days, I hate to say it, but it's true. I would just say to the studio, "I want to do a curtain call, I need an extra day," and they'd say, "fine." If you said it today, unless you're Spielberg, or Scorsese, or maybe Coppola, they'd never even think of letting you do it.

Moscow on the Hudson *made me remember Ayn Rand's testimony before HUAC, insisting that "they never smile in Russia."* Moscow on the Hudson *says the same thing.*

Well, things *are* bad there. I went there with Leon. I got the idea for *Moscow on the Hudson* because I had made *Willie & Phil* and I was lecturing at NYU for the graduate class, and one of the people in the audience asked me what I was doing next, and I said I was going to do *Tempest*, and he asked for a job. He was a Russian, a guy named Vladamir Tukan. He said, "I study camera—assistant cameraman." I said, "I don't have any jobs. I didn't come here with jobs out. You're not in the union, I'm going to Greece." "Take me; I pay my own way." He was so insistent that I told him to come to my office, which was nearby. A couple of days later he showed up and talked me into letting him go. He would sleep on the roof—that was my deal with him—which he was happy to do. And during the course of this journey I tried to talk to him and he told me his story about leaving Russia, and trying to get out of the army by leaping from a window. He only broke his leg, and he couldn't really hurt himself enough. He told me about someone who defected who had been in an orchestra, and defected in a department store. And I suddenly saw a movie. It's funny how you get these ideas. In mine, a guy's gonna defect in Bloomingdale's. That's all I knew. So I made him a circus musician and I came up with this thing and got hold of Leon and we started plotting and writing it. We did a lot of interviews with, say, ten or fifteen Russians who had come to America—they hadn't defected, really, but had somehow gotten out. A couple of jazz musicians even. We wrote the script together, and when the script was finished, I decided we had to go to Russia. We had a "go" picture by now, but I had to go to Russia to see, "Is this accurate?" The first twenty pages were set in Russia.

We went—it's a complicated story, which I won't tell you, but it was grim There were lines, and people were running to get onto them and they didn't even know what the line was for. Maybe it's a cantaloupe. Maybe it's underwear. Maybe it's toilet paper. They needed everything at that time, which was 1980. I was followed by the KGB, I know it[38]. But we felt validated that the script was on the money. For me the great discovery was making everybody in it an immigrant. The lawyer was Latino, the girl is Italian, he is Russian, he meets Russians, Chinese, the Jamaican in the INS office, there's an Iranian—that's America. It's about my grandparents when they came; everybody was an immigrant. And Robin [Williams] was great.

It isn't really a sad film. It's also very patriotic without waving flags.

Well, it is sad, because when you've met his grandfather and his family and all that, he leaves it to come here and be a dishwasher.

---

38 A friendly Russian seconded himself to Mazursky during the latter's stay, and only afterwards did Mazursky realize that he "guide" was probably KGB.

After he defects, when he tells Connie Chung how happy he is to be here, he's crying, but physically he's smiling.

That was a great moment.

As his friend Anatoly (Elya Baskin) pulls away with the departing Russians, probably to a gulag, aboard **Liberty Bus Lines.**

There's a lot of that. I always felt that Robin's managers had very mixed feelings about doing it. I showed it to them. Robin seems to like it a lot. His managers, I don't know. You can print this, I don't care. I never felt that they were thrilled. I don't know what they were after.

Didn't you first approach Mikhail Baryshnikov?

Yes.

And Dustin Hoffman, too.

Yes.

And also that you got Robin Williams to learn Russian.

Yes, which he did in three months. Amazing. I also approached Alexander Gudinov, who I quite liked, and he only wanted to play the main part. I wanted him to play the clown part. Luckily, he didn't do it, and I got Elya Baskin. Gudinov kept asking, "Why can't I play it?" and I said, "Because I need a star. You're not a star." He was a great dancer. He died very young. He was very smart and very nice. Sad. I liked him a lot.

Robin Williams has his fans and his detractors. Except for your film and **Good Morning, Vietnam** *he has never seemed genuine to me.*

I don't know. I liked him in *Good Will Hunting*. I liked him in *Good Morning, Vietnam*. He's a big, big talent—at times bigger than life—very bright. And he's odd. I think if he could resist being loved in a part, he'd be better off. His weakness is to play roles of people who are noble. Listen, you can't make as many moves as some of these guys make and click all the time. I'm not here to criticize it. He did everything I wanted. We had our first couple of meetings after he agreed to do *Moscow on the Hudson*. I thought he was doing schtick when we were in Russia (actually shot in Munich, Germany) and I said, "You don't have to do all that. Do it straight, simple; don't be funny." But that's not trouble, that's normal. He was wonderful, and he was wonderful to the other actors. It wasn't like he was a star.

Did you rewrite any of the dialogue to accommodate his speech patterns?

No. My main thing in directing is to leave people alone when they're doing it right. The only time I start interfering is when they're not doing it right or I feel they could be doing it better.

Your script begins with 20 or 25 pages in Russian. The film, however, begins in English in America.

Frank Price, who paid for this script, and for the movie (the movie cost 12.5, I think) said, "We got a real problem. Your first 20 pages are subtitled and 83 percent of the audience can't read." He had some number that high. So I said, "Let me try to come up with a solution." And I finally came up with it.

So you added the opening scene on a New York City bus where Vlad gives explicit directions to a more recent immigrant.

Which is in English, and the film becomes a flashback. Then we made the clown (Elya Baskin) someone who speaks in English because he's defecting, so he's learned English. So now we have scenes of them in English. So the only scenes that are only in Russian are between him and the grandfather, Aleksandr Benyaminov, who's a great actor. The KGB guy (Saveli Kramarov) speaks English, too.

You've spoken of the unusual method of filming certain scenes on location.

Yes, we shot night for day. Usually you shoot day for night. We shot night for day.

Please explain that.

When we scouted the Bavaria Studios, which we used because it had the trolley line that had been built for Bergman for *The Serpent's Egg*—when he was kicked out of Sweden for taxes—we had scouted in the winter when it was snowing. I didn't go there, Pato, my production designer, went there. And Pato said it would work. When we got to shoot the movie, we shot in the summertime when it stays light all day and there is very little night, because it's Germany, and the farther north you go, the more light. Secondly, it was so sunny and so hot, we couldn't make it look like Moscow, which is grim and gray and the lights are on in the streets at 11 in the morning. So we decided to shoot it at night and pretend it was daytime. You'll never know. It's just darker and the lamps are on and it's daytime. But it's night. It was a German crew; you just tell them what to do and give them more beer and wienerschnitzel and they'll do it. They called me Mien Führer. I said, "Fellas, you can't call me Führer."

Anatoly (Baskin) had a great line in the hotel room where Vlad (Williams) is busy stealing toilet paper. He said, "You should care less about your ass and more about your soul." That's a line that describes the whole film.

I still see Elya Baskin a lot. He's wonderful. And he still sees Robin; Robin's remained loyal. Elya was very disappointed because, in the sequel we wrote, he had a very good part. In the sequel[39], Robin's character is now a Yuppie. He's got all these people in the park selling toys, they work for him. They're Indian, Pakistani, and he treats them like shit. He's got a loft in SoHo, he's got lots of women, he's got a BMW that says "Vlad." He's doing great but he's got one problem: he has no more soul. The Russian thing is gone. He gets a call in the middle of the night from Russia and it's his mother telling him that his sister is getting married and he's got to come to the wedding. He's terribly afraid to come back, but he goes back to Russia. The clown, Elya, is now a top black market guy and picks him up in a limo. He meets a woman doctor and falls in love. They have a great affair. Then it's time for him to go back to America and she won't go with him. He asks, "How can you stay here?" She says, "This is my country." So we reverse the other film's problem with the defection. I won't tell you the solution. The solution could maybe be a little better, but it was very good and should have been done. That was another blow. I gave Robin *Moscow on the Rocks*, which only would be done if he did it. He didn't want to do it. That's another great script. How much could it cost? Even if he gets twenty [million]. Not sixty! I don't make movies like that. Onward. I can't answer it.

But let's talk about money. Your next film was Down and Out in Beverly Hills. That was the first Touchstone film, and it made a fortune.

Yes. I wrote *Down and Out* with Leon. Originally the idea was going to be financed by Columbia, and at the last second they backed out. I could have sued them, but I said the hell with it, so we went to Frank Price at Universal and they paid us to do the script. We wrote the script. He liked it very much but he wanted a different ending. He wanted something more like the Nick Nolte character going off with the girl. I didn't buy that. I like Frank very much because Frank financed *Tempest*, *Moscow on the Hudson* and *The Pickle*. I will be eternally grateful to Frank; I like him a lot. But he just had this thing in his head. So my agents said, "Look,

---

39 *Moscow on the Rocks* (q.v.)

there's a new company starting, it's called Touchstone, Michael Eisner and Jeff Katzenberg are leaving Paramount. I think everyone in town's going to want a bite of this project but I think they [Touchstone] will really back it and give you freedom and sell it good." So I went with them. And they were great.

The film went into production with the title Jerry Saved From Drowning.

Jerry Saved From Drowning is based on *Boudu Saved From Drowning* (Jean Renoir, 1932)[40]. It's quite a wonderful movie. The prints you see of it are so old, but Michel Simon is great. I'd seen it when I was in my early twenties at the Museum of Modern Art, so when I got the idea for *Down and Out*, I lived on Alpine Drive in Beverly Hills and it had alleys where I'd go to put the garbage out. One day I was putting the garbage out and I saw a bum, a hobo, a homeless guy, whatever you want to call him, pushing a supermarket cart with a little dog in it. I said, "My God, what if that guy is like the vagabond in *Boudu*—*clochard*, they called him—and instead of jumping in the Seine he jumps in a pool. That was the idea; I had it like that (snaps his fingers). So I got hold of the movie and I called Leon and told it to him and we looked at the movie and we said, "God, it's gonna work." We switched it.

In Boudu the man who saves him owns a bookstore. Jerry is saved by Richard Dreyfuss, who owns a wire clothes hanger factory.

I wanted to make it very specific: a hanger factory. Something more *bourgeois*. More money than he knew what to do with. *Noveau riche*. I wanted to satirize myself, I wanted to satirize Beverly Hills. My wife's not like Bette's [Bette Midler] character and I'm not like Richard's, but aspects of us. I had two kids, two girls; I gave Richard a boy and a girl. In *Boudu* there are no children,

---

40 Vagrant Michel Simon, despondent at the loss of his dog, jumps in the Seine to drown, but is rescued by a bookstore owner who brings him to his home. Simon, in turn, seduces every woman in the house, finally faking his suicide to escape the bourgeois lifestyle he has acquired.

there's a maid, and the maid I kept and made her a revolutionary. All that is original, but the idea came from *Boudu*.

Simon's Boudu is far more of a reprobate than Jerry is.

Jerry's a liar.

But he's not mean, he just tells people what they want to hear.

Ah, he tells them what they want to hear—but he also seduces the guy's wife, he seduces the guy's daughter. He's out there. He's not Mr. Nice. I wouldn't trust him.

But they do invite him into their home at the end.

They do, and the last shot of the movie, when Richard Dreyfuss looks around, at the last second he did a brilliant thing, which is, "What have I done?" (laughs).

And then there's a Buñuellian moment that you put in, which isn't in the script, which is of another homeless guy coming down the street.

Yes, I got a guy, and as the end titles are over, if you stay to see it, this guy, if he has any luck, someone is going to take him in. This is the solution for our society. That doesn't mean that they have to live with us, but we have to embrace the poor. And the squares that we saw in the movie—like the *L.A. Weekly* or *Reader*, someone said, "It's like stepping in dog shit, this movie, how dare they make fun of the homeless this way?" Some moronic thing. I don't want to make one of those movies where you see how bad the homeless life is; *you saw it in this movie!* He's out there eating dog food. He's picking his feet and cleaning it. We saw a whole barrage of homeless people at the beginning. It's a rotten, miserable life. And Jerry decides to kill himself. You don't kill yourself unless it's a miserable life. Christ almighty, didn't they get it?

One of the things that mitigates in favor of Jerry's character is that he's smart, he's got some education, he may be a good con man, he's not on drugs, he's not on alcohol—

He has been on everything, probably. The story that Nick told in the movie, by the way, about the draft and beating it, that's *his* story. He put that in so he'd have something. And then the trainer of the dog, when I told him I wanted the dog to put his chin on Nick's knee and look up, he said, "Mike [the celebrated dog] wouldn't do that." I said, "Why not?" He said, "Because he knows he's lying." I said, "You mean your dog knows when someone's lying?" He says, "Yeah." And I realized I'm dealing with a Method Dog.

Did Mike the dog and Tonto the cat ever work out a deal picture?

Tonto was one of my favorites. He was really like a cat in that you never could totally win him over. Tonto was independent the way cats are. Mike the dog could at least pretend that he loved you. He was a wonderful dog. It's one of my favorite movies. Of all the movies I made, probably the most successful at the box office were *Bob & Carol*, *An Unmarried Woman* and *Down and Out in Beverly Hills*. *Down and Out* today would be the equivalent of at least 100 million. I never made movies because I wanted to make a lot of money, but you always hope they will. When you finish them, like *Alex in Wonderland*, you know it's not going to make a lot of money. But I thought *Down and Out* might, and it did, and I thought we made some important comments about a lot of things in a way that was successful with a lot of people. The masses got it. It's hard to do both.

Between the production design, which was splendid in that film—

Pato and I went to about fifty Beverly Hills nightmare homes. Every one we'd go to, people thought we were praising them; we'd say, "This is fabulous!" And we put together this house, which we built. The outside of the house in the daytime is a real house in

Beverly Hills. The inside of the house is all built on the lot at Disney, and the helicopter [police response to burglar alarm] shots at night were done at Universal's back lot at night where we only built the front of the house. Three different places.

Fooled me.

Fools everybody.

Dave Whiteman's journey is very important because it is, of course, the journey that we should all be making toward recognizing our place in life. Plus the fact that the film marked Richard's and Bette's professional comebacks—

Oh, it's touching. And I anticipated a lot of stuff, such as when I had all those Chinese there, doing business with China. That's way back. Little did I know I'd go to China 14 years later to make a movie with the Chinese.

The massage scene where Nick brings Bette through a whole gamut of emotions. It's physical comedy, it's performance, it's tense, it's funny. She's all over the place.

She did it very well. I knew I was in great shape because I had the dog to cut to. The guy trained the dog to do that [covering its eyes, writhing, etc.]. Bette said to me, "No matter what I do, that fuckin' dog's gonna get all the laughs." And the dog got big laughs. One of my favorite laughs in the movie is when she has her orgasm and all that stuff goes on, and you cut to Little Richard[41] who goes, "Woooo!" Little Richard was great.

While working on Down and Out, did Bette Midler and Little Richard jam?

---

41 The flamboyant pop singer Little Richard plays the flamboyant next-door neighbor

At the party when the movie was over they jammed. We had a party in the back where the pool was and he played the piano and he sang. A little bit.

Mark Rydell once described Bette to me as "a shy little Jewish girl from Honolulu." When I told her what he'd said, she smiled back at me and said, "Oh he did? I'll kill him!" She has such a brassy image, but she's wonderfully ditzy in Down and Out.

Bette's a very giving person. Her nervousness early-on was, "Is this funny? Should I do more? Shouldn't it be bigger? We're not doing anything?" And I said, "Bette, you don't have to do much. You are funny. The minute I see you, I'm ready to laugh. I can't help it." And Richard was very supportive and Nick was very supportive and there was never any trouble. But she needed the support. Had she been an egomaniac, I might have made changes that would have hurt it. I never had to. And she came up with some great stuff, like when she had her nails painted and she tapped them on the Mercedes while she was driving. That's fabulous. What I'm talking about, about making changes, is how can it *not* happen? I can criticize myself as director and say I've been slavishly faithful to the studios in trying to bring pictures in on time, where, let's take a guy like Kubrick, long may he rest, Stanley never worried about that. He may have had a 52 day schedule and when he hit the 100th day, he didn't really know he was hitting the 100th day. Charlie Chaplin used to stop shooting. But he owned the studio. Things don't always work. And maybe some of the movies that we see could be better if they waited, but they can't do that sort of thing any more.

Reading the script, it didn't look as if you changed it at all when you got to the floor.

I didn't. I rehearsed all the scenes that take place in the house in the set and showed it to the cameraman, production designer, the key grip, sound man, hair and makeup. I showed about twenty people. We kept moving around set to set, all day, all the scenes.

It all worked. We knew we had a winner from the rehearsal. I wanted Bette, Richard, and Nick to feel that fullness. Sure, they blew a line here or there, but it was great, and it made me feel secure in how we we're gonna shoot it. I would run around and say, "We're gonna be over here" and "we're gonna be over there."

And they had the timing from rehearsals.

Yes, and then it got even better. It gave them the security to know they weren't operating in the dark. They were making people laugh. You can't make a film crew laugh, take it from me. They're all too concerned about the jobs they do being correct. They were on the floor.

They say comedy doesn't work in close-up, only two-shot. Is that true?

Depends on what kind of comedy. If it's physical comedy, you generally want to see the body. If it's a look you're into, a close-up's gonna work. When Bette and Richard are in bed and he's watching the son's video and she has her eye shades on and she lifts up the patch off of one eye and gives that look, that's a fairly tight shot of her going, "Jesus Christ." One of my favorite shots is where I used the widest angle lens to show them in bed trying to get cozy, and I used the wide angle lens to make the bed and the room look like a house. It's not very comforting. You know, one of the problems with the *noveau riche* is that they really don't have very good taste, they don't know what to do with the money, et cetera.

Isn't there some French law involving droit morale **that says that if you're going to remake a film, you have to get the original film-maker's permission? You credit the play, not Renoir's film.**

I had to go back to the play, which was a boulevard comedy by René Fauchois, *Boudu sauvé des eaux*. I called it *Jerry Saved From Drowning*, and then I realized that title was going to get us in a lot of trouble because nobody was going to go see it, and then we came up with *Down and Out in Beverly Hills*. The French writer is very protected. The Writers Guild of America is always looking for that kind of protection.

Very few American films examine marriages. They focus on the romance leading up to it, and divorce resulting from it, but rarely an ongoing marriage. Yours do.

I wrote about what I knew. I knew about the middle class. From my own experience, I knew about the lower middle-class, *Next Stop, Greenwich Village*. Bad marriage, in a way, between my mother and father, which was not portrayed too bad, except she clearly was the boss and he was the quiet, simpler fellow. And then I got into marriage with *Bob & Carol, Blume in Love, Unmarried Woman, Down & Out, Willie & Phil, Tempest*—big time about marriage—not *Moon Over Parador*.

And *not* Moscow on the Hudson.

There's a lot of marriage, no doubt about it. I've been married 48 years and, as I've told lots of people, I've had 27 great years in my marriage, which is pretty good out of 48. No (seriously, folks), it's been great. If you can find a better institution, tell me about it. There's no doubt it presents problems and the values and mores and styles have changed over the years. But marriage is about commitment, and I was always trying to examine it.

You and Leon wrote a sequel to Down and Out. What happened to it?

In the sequel, they lose all their money and they have to move into an apartment. They have to have a garage sale, and Little Richard's character buys most of the stuff to help out. Dave gets a job—finally—at Burger King. It was funny. It was a can't-miss. Well, they passed on it, which is the most flabbergasted I have ever been in all my dealings in movies.

They passed on a sequel to one of the most successful films ever made?

When you see the sequels to movies these days, most of them are unbearable, but they're almost always fairly successful at the box office. And here I had Richard Dreyfuss and Bette lined up—and these morons passed. Quote me. I don't know. I can't explain anything in this world.

There was a TV series, though.

The TV series was based on the original. It was okay but not very good; I had nothing to do with it.. You know, in the original *Boudu* of Renoir, in case you forgot, do you remember how it ends?

He jumps in the river again.

But he doesn't kill himself. He makes it *look* like he killed himself. He ends up floating down the river on his back, free again, a happy man. I couldn't do that, because if you go back on the road to eat dog food, it's not a happy life. In the early 30s, when Renoir made the film, there were vagabonds who wanted this life, and there was something romantic about it. Boudu ended up floating on the water amidst the flowers and trees. It's a fabulous ending. We thought about doing something like that, but it didn't work.

Didn't President Reagan say that some people just like to live outdoors?

Yeah, he did.

Top row: Jill, Steve Cody, Betsy; bottom row Kate, Monza, Snowball, Paul, Carly (Mazursky collection)

Andre Philippe, Paul, Betsy, Meg (Mazursky collection)

Paul's star on Hollywood Boulevard in front of Musso & Frank's, the oldest surviving Hollywood Restaurant

Paul and daughter Jill at Cabo San Lucas (Mazursky collection)

Paul Mazursky directs Jill Clayburgh in this production still from
An Unmarried Woman

Betsy and Paul (Mazursky collection)

Above:
Bob & Carol & Ted & Alice *reunion: Robert Culp, Paul, Dyan Cannon, and Elliott Gould. Missing: Natalie Wood (Mazursky collection)*

Paul with granddaughter Molly on the Oscar® red carpet. At the time, Paul was on the Academy's Board of Governors (Mazursky collection)

Leon Capetanos and Paul (Mazursky collection)

Margot Kidder, Jill Clayburgh, Paul, Dyan Cannon, Natalie Wood at the premiere of Willie and Phil (Mazursky collection)

Paul's directorial debut, Bob & Carol & Ted & Alice

Fear & Desire. *Paul is second from right, bottom row (photo: Virginia Leith, Wiki Commons)*

Fear & Desire

John Cassavetes, Betsy, and Paul making Tempest *(Mazursky collection)*

Margot Kidder, Paul, Ellen Burstyn (photo: Paul Schumach) (Mazursky collection)

Directing Blume in Love *in Venice*

Paul and Betsy in younger days (Mazursky collection)

Alan Bates, Paul, Jill Clayburgh making An Unmarried Woman

Betsy and Paul (yes, it's Paul) making Moon Over Parador *(Mazursky collection)*

With Jill Clayburgh on An Unmarried Woman

Paul with Vic Morrow (right) in The Blackboard Jungle

Betsy memorial card (Mazursky collection)

RIDING HIGH

Nat Segaloff: Moon Over Parador, *like* Down and Out, *is another reinterpretation of an existing film. Had you seen* The Magnificent Fraud[42]?

Paul Mazursky: Yes. That's why I did it. Didn't I tell you this?

No.

Some guy called my office and my secretary at that time said, "There's a weird guy on the phone. He's calling and saying he has the rights to bad movies." That sounded funny, so I said, "Put him on."
"Yes?"
"I have the rights to a lot of movies that were failures but I think have great ideas."
"Tell me one or two."
So he tells me one or two, and they're ridiculous. I'm about to hang up when he says, "Then there's one with Akim Tamiroff"—whom I happen to love—"about a dictator who dies and is impersonated by an actor."
I said, "Come over to my office."
He gives me the film and it's terrible—but it's a great idea. And there's even a couple of moments in it. So I started dreaming and

---

42 Akim Tamiroff plays an actor who poses as a South American dictator. Robert Florey directed Walter Ferris's and Gilbert Gabriel's script from Charles G. Booth's story, 1939. Moreover, since it's a story about an actor who doubles for a dictator, it was convenient that Lorin Dreyfuss so closely resembles his brother, the actor, Richard.

I come up with this thing in my head and I tell the guy, "Look, I have a way of doing this but where do you come in?" "Well, I want to be Associate Producer" and this and that, "and if it works out, I'll get you involved and we'll make a deal out of it" and I got ahold of Leon Capetanos. My idea was basically very close to the movie you saw. Leon loved it, he saw the movie with me, we pitched it together, we went in and talked to, I think, Frank Price, and the next thing you know, we had a script. We had great [location] scouts in Latin America for research and other things.

I went to Guatemala and Salvador—there was a war going on at that time, they had guys up against buses being searched by soldiers. Then I went to Mexico. Where are we gonna shoot it? Finally I found out about this place in Brazil called Ouro Preto. Got a production designer named Marcos Flaksman who lives in Brazil—Pato Guzman knew him—Pato said, "We hear Ouro Preto is magnificent. We need a great plaza for speeches." He said it was perfect; "I'll go there and video it." Which he did, and sent it to us; we looked at it and said, "We gotta go." So Pato and I went and (snaps his fingers) that was it. It was fantastic.

Now we were confronted with, Can we get Universal to make a picture in Brazil, which is very far from their control? They wanted me to go to Mexico City. First of all, there was no plaza in Mexico; their main plaza, Socoro, in Mexico City. But I couldn't stand the idea of working in Mexico City and doing all the studio work there, because I couldn't breathe. I literally had trouble breathing in Mexico City, the air was so bad. So we said, "Look, we'll do it in Brazil" and made a budget. Which they agreed. It was hard. But I gotta give them credit.

We then cast the picture and I had a fabulous time making it. We shot it in Rio de Janeiro, where we did certain things—the Opera House for the interiors and all those ballroom scenes, where I play the mother and go up and down those stairs. That was modeled after the Paris Opera House. Then we had a studio we found—an abandoned factory that made paper clips or something—and Pato turned it into a studio. We had to air condition it and put in soundproofing. He built all these sets. The thing about *Moon Over Parador* is that we combined three places to make this movie work: interiors all built of the palace except the Opera House; exteriors, a coupe of odd places in Rio near water for drive-ups and going in; and then in Ouro Preto all of the stuff that's supposed to be the plaza, the parades. The plaza takes place outside the palace. The palace was in Rio and in the studio. The interiors were in Ouro Preto, plus parades, and a few other things. The driving shots were live driving near the plaza. We combined that and Salvador, which is another place we found, where I shot the scenes with Jonathan Winters walking down the street and into—

— the cafe with the umbrellas and the cocktails—

— cocktails, all that is in Salvador. Salvador is like a place called Bahia, a section of Brazil, and if you ever go to Brazil, try to make it your business to go to Salvador. It's intense and it's wonderful. It's Africa and Latin America and all of it combined with a pulse and a beat and music and food. It's devastating. Anyway, we made it all, and it was a miracle. Pato did it for peanuts. The movie cost money. It wasn't dirt-cheap. It cost about 18 million probably.

Which is nothing. I also haven't seen Richard that endearing since **The Goodbye Girl.**

He was great.

I had forgotten about his brother, Lorin, who did much of the doubling.

Yeah. That's his brother.

How did you get all the extras in the square. Was that the eighteen million dollars on the screen?

Minas Gerais is a mining town, and they have samba schools. They work all year, and after they work in the mines the go to samba school, and then they meet several times a week and create costumes for a Mardi Gras they have every year. We hired six thousand of them—it cost $7 a person—it cost me about 60 or 70 Gs. Peanuts. But here's the funny thing. We hire about five or six thousand, it's a big plaza, packed, as you saw, and an extra two or three thousand showed up wanting to do it, who didn't get paid! So I used them. There were 8,000 extras.

Meanwhile Universal is seeing dailies and thinking that's where their money was going.

Oh, they liked it. When they see large crowds—it was magnificent. Universal, they were okay. They were always complaining about the cost of napkins.

Did you get to keep your wardrobe[43]?

No. Have I told you that story?

It's in your book—about Judith Malina [co-founder of The Living Theatre with Julian Beck].

She was heartbroken on the phone in Germany. It was an opera, I think, that she was doing for a high school or junior college in Germany. I said, "Let her out for four days. That's all this will take. She flies—ba-boom, ba-baam..." "Not ze ziggen-zei hot-sen..." (German double-talk, meaning "no way."). You know, I saw Rene (Reinhard) Kolldehoff on television a few nights ago in some excruciating movie with William Holden about spies in Holland during the Second World War. Rene is the German guy who played the German guy [Dieter Lopez]. I hired him based on the way he looked—a fabulous-looking man and a good actor—but by he time he showed up to do the movie, he'd had major heart trouble and couldn't remember any of his lines. *Any of them.*

"I can do eet, Paul—pleece! Let me finish!"

"All right, Rene. Action!"

---

43 When actress Judith Malina was unable to play the role of the dictator's mother, Mazursky did it—in drag.

"Zo nice to zee you, my—my—oh, Gott in himmel, vat iss de vords?"

"Cut. Rene, just don't say 'Gott in himmel.' If you forget the lines, just do it anyway. Action."

"Zo nice to see you, my dicta-ta-ta-ta...oy, vat, hoo-hoo, Gott in himmel..."

"Cut!"

I said, "Rene, I'm gonna say the line to you and you repeat it! 'So nice to see you, my dictator'."

"Zo nice to zee you my dictator!"

"Cut, print!"

It meant a lot to him, I'm sure.

It did. It did. A great face. And Fernando Rey, who had several scenes with him—Fernando is certainly one of the two or three greatest guys I ever worked with. I treat him, not just with kid gloves, but with divine adoration—I mean, he was in the Luis Buñuel films. We had a few days of rehearsal, and one day he says to me [flawless Spanish accent], "Paul, I know that you have nothing but the greatest respect for me."

I said, "Well, I do, Fernando."

"Nevertheless, I would appreciate it if you would treat me like the dog, cur, actor that I am. Just shout out to me what to do."

It must have been a happy shoot, then.

It was a lot of fun. No real trouble. In spite of the mechanics. And look who I had: Sammy Davis, Jr. and Jonathan Winters in the same hotel in Ouro Preto where Sammy's luggage was mostly in the hallway because he had 22 pieces and the room was about the size of this room (15x30), a little bit bigger. He said to me, "Kid, how could you do this to me? I can't even get my luggage in the room." He was a great guy.

Raul Julia's characterization is different in the film than it's written in the script. He's much crazier. At what point did you change it?

Well, I'd always had that in mind; to me it's there. I told him to dye his hair blond, which he did—the only way we could justify the whole thing: he's a Nazi. And it worked. This was a man who was capable of killing. That's all there is to it. So you might say, well, Jeez, I'll get out of this thing. But you have to go along with it or he'll kill you. And Raul was wonderful. My favorite line in the movie—and one of my favorites of any movie of mine—is his dying line, "I hate actors." He was angry, crazy and charming.

All at the same time.

Raul was a really great actor. A man who could do musical comedy, farce, Shakespeare tragedy, serious work, Latino—he could do it all. Raul's biggest thing, though, was that he was always looking for the part that had nothing Latin about it. So he was kind of pissed at me, years later, when I had *Pictures of Fidelman*, which I never got made, about a Jewish painter in New York. He wanted to play it.

He said, "How come I can't do it?"
I said, "Raul, you're too Latin—oops!"
"I could play a Jew."
And maybe he could.

Scene 69—which is, fittingly, the sex scene between Jack (Richard Dreyfuss) and Madonna (Sonia Braga)—is a lot tamer on film than in the script. Was it cut for a PG-13?

No, but I don't think I did that as well as I could've. I think it could have been hotter. It certainly wasn't the fault of Sonia. It was tricky. I don't think it's my best piece of work, to be quite candid with you. I think if I had it to do over I should have done the scene again and made it—first of all, the room should have been darker. It should have been difficult to see faces; it was over-lit.

Secondly, it was too comical with Richard's moustache going off-kilter. But once they got past that it was great. I bought it all, but it could have been better.

You're talking about a deception, and then a deception on top of a deception.

It's a farce, but I wanted it to be believable.

That raises an interesting question of how far you can milk the gag. The audience knows the set-up when they buy their ticket, so how much can you play with that and not bore the audience?

When the studio saw this movie they were scared. If I remember, Tom Pollack, who was running the studio then, and is a nice man, was hoping that I would take out all the New York stuff and have no flashbacks, which I wouldn't do. What the movie is about—and it has several levels of what it's about—is the fact that Ronald Reagan was our president. Actors become President of the United States of America! An actor is such a desperate human being that he'll do anything to play a part. *Anything*. One of the great scenes is when Richard's brought into the meat locker where the dead dictator is hanging on a hook—it's a great scene if I say so myself—and he's trying to get out because this madman, Raul, is crazy and is beating up the dead dictator for dying—and Richard wants to escape, but then Raul starts reading him his reviews. That's enough to keep any actor back in the room; he even adds, "By the way, they left out..." Richard did that magnificently. Some of the scenes between Fernando Rey and Richard, where Ray is suspecting the masquerade but says nothing, were quite wonderful. So the movie's about deception, role-playing, all of that stuff. It was a tricky movie because it has all these layers. And it's framed by an actor who's waiting to go in for an audition telling these guys, "You ever hear of Parador?" And then one of Maurice Jarre's great scores—and there's this miraculous place—well, to do it without New York was just a joke.

You have to get to know the actor first and actors' desperation—

Of course. The first scene there [in Parador where Dreyfuss is shooting a movie on location] where he's playing the guy in the white suit and all the over-acting and the stunt where he falls over the railing—

With Michael Greene playing the stunt coordinator, who later returns to help Richard escape—it's perfect symmetry.

All of that was stolen from us—and you can print every word I say here—whether it was stolen consciously or not I can't say to you—but the movie *Dave*[44]—it's all out of this. I went to Pollack because I had read *Dave* and I said, "Look, how can it be a coincidence changing bodies in an ambulance and this and this and the other—"
And they said, "The guy never saw *Moon Over Parador*."
I said, "But *you* guys see it. How can you—?"
"Well, I have a deal with Ivan Reitman. Forget about it." *Dave* was a pretty good movie, but I was angry, 'cause our stuff was way before this, and *Dave* was a hit and ours wasn't, and Kevin Kline was very good. That movie was much softer. The romance was more treacly.

Moon Over Parador *was your first real foray into political satire per se.* You had always been more at home in social satire.

Yes. I put my politics in through the story. In this one, I had scenes in the so-called *favellas* where they're burning and this and that, and somebody wrote one review—it's the only one I remember—of me "making light" of the terrible problems in Latin America. You can't win!

What's in a Poona besides rum?

---

44 *Dave* (dir. Ivan Reitman; scr. Gary Ross; Warner Bros., 1993) stars Kevin Kline as a Washington, DC businessman recruited by devious White House aides to substitute for a corrupt, stroke-felled president.

The drink that they serve in Brazil is called a Caipirinha, and Caipirinha is made from sugar cane alcohol (cachaca). The drink is the alcohol of sugar canes and a lot of limes and a lot of sugar and ice. It's served in rather smallish glasses, and when you get it, you think it's a kind of a mild Margarita. I would say that one small Caipirinha is enough to put you away for an hour and a half, and two, forget it. And I had a lot of Caipirinhas in Brazil. I was in social situations where I just couldn't refuse. I hardly drink, but it's so sweet, it's delicious.

There are no virgin Caipirinhas in Brazil.

So "Poona," we just made up. There's a Poona mug [points to the sideboard in his office]. Pato was one of the greatest production designers in the world, who never got an award. He created everything right down to the stationery of the palace. He was a magician and had a great sense of cinema. He would build just enough to use to cut to the next scene, but didn't have to build the whole room. [Sighs] Pato was my brother[45].

Maurice Jarre was an unusual choice for you as composer. He also did Enemies, A Love Story. He's better known for symphonic scores than the source music required for Parador.

We wanted to create a sound that was unique and distinctly Paradorian. And since there's no such place as Parador, he took the liberty of using all kinds of Latin music and elevating it one step so that it had a kind of class, as opposed to the lower street music. It's a very good score, and he's played it all over the world with symphonies when he conducts. By the way, the first time Maurice saw the movie—I had some temporary music in it—he's on the floor. When it's over, he says to me—I'd never met him—[perfect French accent], "What a most unusual, deleecious, charrrming, funny feelm. And the actors, zey are breelliant. But even zough zey are all breeliant—Raul, what ees hees name, Joolia—

---
[45] Pato Guzman died in 1991 after a brief illness. He had designed 11 of Mazursky's films, beginning with *I Love You, Alice B. Toklas*. He was 58.

and Braga—who is zee actress who plays zee mother of Reechard Dreyfuss?"

I said, "Oh, Carlotta Gerson, an Argentinean actress I was lucky enough to meet when I was down in Rio."

"She ees breeliant! Breeliant!"

And I put my face right next to Maurice and said, "Do you really think so, Maurice?"

"Yes!"

"Would you like me to tell her?"

"Yes."

"Why don't you tell her yourself?"

"Where can I find her?"

I said, [doing Mamma], "She's right here, next to you!" Well, he almost fainted. It was a great moment for me.

And Carlotta's name is in the credits, of course, not yours.

I put "her" name in the credits. A lot of people didn't know it was me.

I had a continuity question. Madonna is supposed to be either sent out of the country or killed; instead, she stays. Doesn't she recognize the threat against her? How does she feel safe enough to stay when she knows that it's her death?

I think she knows that the people are with her. The only danger would come from Roberto (Raul Julia). Then, in the last scene on the balcony, when she's making that final speech—by the way, most of the people with her up there are townspeople from Ouro Preto; they loved it. I was the kind of Ouro Preto for four weeks. One of the things that happened was, for whatever reason, we had, every single morning, this unbearable fog, mist, and even rainfall—light, but rainfall—and they would always say to me, "You can't shoot outside today, it's going to be raining." And I would do a funny rain dance that I made up and, sure enough, about 10:15 the sun would come out and they would start screaming, "Ma-zur-sky! Ma-zur-sky!" They had great names for me. It was so much fun, Jesus.

How do you direct Jonathan Winters?

With alacrity. He's very smart. His big thing is, he's a big guy, and he was pretty uncomfortable in the car scenes—"God damn car's got springs up my ass"—and it must have been a hundred degrees, I'm not joking, and we're towing him along and I'd say, "Cut, let's do it again." He was fun. He's a wonderful guy.

He's an experience. The asides, facial expressions—

I told him, "Jonathan, don't worry about the lines. Say them if you can, but if something strikes you, say it." So he threw in things that I wanted.

You put other things in the film, such as having Richard do the Ronald Reagan wave to the press as he walks to the noisy helicopter and pretends not to hear their questions.

There's a lot of stuff like that. What drove me crazy was—have I told you the story of the first preview?

No.

As you do, I showed the film to the studio, to Tom Pollack and a couple of other people, and they really seemed to like it. Then we decided to have a preview in Dallas, Texas. Very tough town to preview a sophisticated movie but, what the hell, I can take it. So they fly all of us in on a private jet to Dallas. My agent, Sam Cohn comes. We get to the theatre around 7 or 7:30 for an 8 o'clock screening, and there's hardly anybody in the theatre. I'm starting to say to myself, "Nobody knows who Richard Dreyfuss is? Who Paul Mazursky is?" Well, I find out that the Dallas NBA team is playing the Lakers that night. It's a 500 seat theatre and there's only 200 people. How can you preview a comedy in a theatre that's more than half-empty? But they went and did it, and I think I paid for it forever. They laugh, but they're scared, and when it was over we had this unbearable meeting where they're all telling me to cut it, changed this, do that. I said, "What happened to the movie you loved?" They said, "Well, the audience..." I said, "That's not an audience." I did a few things to it; they previewed it again; by now the opening was delayed by six weeks or something, the preview for Universal was much better, but they lost their faith in the picture and it wasn't advertised in the right way. Maybe it was too hip for the room, I don't know. But it's become a cult favorite and people come up to me all the time and quote lines from it, like "What a great day for a speech." Like "show me the magic" from *Tempest*.

ISAAC BASHEVIS SINGER, A LOVE STORY

Nat Segaloff: Enemies, A Love Story[46] *is Jewish cinema versus non-Jewish cinema. When does Jewish cinema become mainstream cinema?*

Paul Mazursky: Well, I don't see it as Jewish cinema. I see *Enemies, A Love Story* as a great novel by a great writer who happens to be Jewish. Of course, I identify with a lot of feelings in it, even though I am an atheist. But I'm Jewish. And I feel very attached to things Jewish culturally, and very confused about certain other things, and I can tear up very easily when my granddaughter came home from the school she goes to—my granddaughter's father is Irish-Italian-American and her mother, my daughter, is half-Jewish, and the little kid happens to be going to a little Hebrew school called the Leo Beck school for three-year-olds. She came home and I said, "What did you learn today, Molly?" And she said, "Oh, today we learned some songs." (singing in ersatz Hebrew) "Shoyvel a hoim vella heem meeneyvoh," and she started to sing some of these Hebrew songs. Well, a big tear started to roll down the right eye.

Singer is a great writer and one of the big frustrations of my career has been not being able to make *Shosha*, (NY: Farrar, Straus, Giroux, 1978) which is another great Singer book that I had

---

46 Herman Broder (Ron Silver), who survived the Holocaust by hiding in a hayloft under the protection of a slow-witted Polish girl Yadwiga (Margaret Sophie Stein), marries her and comes to America, settling in Brooklyn in 1949. He also marries his mistress, Masha (Lena Olin) who lives in the Bronx. Then his first wife, Tamara (Anjelica Huston), whom he thought had died in the camps, shows up.

the rights to and I couldn't find the money. But *Enemies* is a great novel and that's why I did it. I didn't do it to promote how brave the Jews were, but I did it hoping to understand that Jews were sexual, sensual and all of the other stuff that we're used to seeing the goyim do: affairs, cheating, lying, everything. It's a fantastic book and, you know, luckily I was able to, with Roger Simon, come up with a script that left out about at least a third of the book.

You've matched the sensuality on screen that Singer is able to get into his words.

Singer's never too explicit; the old man didn't do that. I showed the movie at the one and only Moscow Jewish Film Festival and the people saw it under very difficult conditions. There's no subtitles. It was an English language version, and a woman sits in the back, who's seen the picture in the morning, and that night she does a simultaneous translation into a microphone. So while the movie is playing in English, with the music and everything, and the actors are speaking fairly loudly, but not quite as loud as it would be projected in a theatre, you're hearing a woman in a microphone going (flawless Russian accent) "Glorshni petista durkin—Herman." "Vlibbed dey—Masha." It was killing me!

When the lights came on, and they were devastated by the picture, one guy told me, "I went to jail for you. I saw *Moscow on the Hudson* in a pirated videotape and they caught me and I was in jail. And I want to thank you for what you've done for us. And he took off his Russian Army wristwatch and handed it to me.

I said, "I can't take this, sir."

He said, "You have to take it!"

So I took it. I get back to the hotel, and it doesn't work. That's my metaphor for Russia.

There's an undercurrent of "Survivors Guilt" that runs through the story, which is apparently quite rife among concentration camp survivors and those who had no direct connection with the Holocaust but question why they were permitted to live while others were not.

I'll tell you who has guilt: survivors' children. I got close to a couple of the children who are your age (50) and sometimes younger. In order for Anjelica Huston could get a feel for Jewishness, I found a Hungarian woman who arranged for a *shabbas* (Sabbath) dinner, a Friday night dinner, with ten Hungarian survivors. My wife and I, Anjelica, and this group of Hungarians. Fantastic experience. They were all survivors. Most of them, by the way, were much less depressed than you'd think. They didn't show it, anyway. One was very angry and down, kinda crazed, but the rest were charming, they were funny. Over the period of time that I was rehearsing in New York, I would take Lena Olin, Anjelica and even Margaret Stein to Jewish restaurants on the lower east side. One day one of the waiters was asking what we wanted and he was wearing a short-sleeved white shirt, and there were the numbers. Well, that did more for the preparation than anything. They looked at a lot of movies, I had them read a lot of Yiddish stuff, documentary footage, and it was an education for me, too. But I'm shocked and always have been, and amazed, at the courage of most of those people. It's overwhelming.

For decades, Hollywood resisted making films about Jews. How were you able to get Enemies made?

I got interested in that book in 1970 and I tried to get Dustin Hoffman interested and I got no response. I forgot about it and over the years I would write, I would make a movie, smell around a little bit if anyone was interested in *Enemies*, get nowhere, do another movie, till finally I did *Down and Out in Beverly Hills* for Disney and they liked it so much, they were so happy, and they underpaid me so much that they felt guilty, and they said, "Sure, *Enemies*, do it." We optioned the book and they paid for a screenplay, but I don't think they knew what it was. The way I pitched it was a comedy about guy with three wives. Then they read the script and they shit.

It was like, "Jesus Christ, does it have to be this? Does it have to be that?"

I said, "Yes it does."

"Can't you update it?" That's what Michael Eisner said to me.

"I said, 'it's pretty hard to update the Holocaust, Michael, unless you want me to set it in Cambodia and have it in New York with Cambodians here living in...'"

But I got to make it, and it's one of the great joys of my life. And I must confess that, after I made that movie, I made *Scenes from a Mall* and had total control and I got to make *The Pickle* which is a movie I predict will be re-appreciated as years go by, and from then on it became very difficult to get financing for the kind of scripts that I like. So *Enemies* is kind of the top of the mountain. It was very well reviewed, even by Stanley Kauffmann, who wrote something like, "Who would have thought that Mazursky, who has given us such dreadful things as so-and-so, could have come up with a masterpiece?"

It certainly is an atypical film for you.

People can say that, but, look: it's Singer. It's me interpreting Singer, but it's Singer. Yes, it's atypical in that I've never written about that, but if you look at *Next Stop, Greenwich Village*, there are some Singer Jews in there. The mother, the father—there's a little bit of it in there. If you're looking for misery and terror and profound problems in people's lives, it's in *Harry & Tonto*, it's in *Blume in Love*. It's even in *Willie & Phil*. There are dark things in this movie, and these are dark movies.

You and Roger Simon flipped the ending so that the movie winds up on an appropriate and more upbeat tone than the book.[47]

The book, to me, was so open-ended that I had no idea. I wasn't really sure, and I read it ten times. I had originally written, with Roger, a scene in Miami where Herman is writing this letter in a

---

47 Singer ends his novel with a hurried, two-page epilogue in which Herman disappears, Masha's suicide is discovered, and Yadwiga has Herman's child, which the rabbi suggests be named Masha. The film places Herman in Florida from where he mails $20 in child support, and makes Yadwiga's and Tamara's decision their own to name Herman's child Masha. The beats are similar, but the film offers a more emotional resolution.

motel around a pool, one of those Miami dumps, and he's typing the letter which she later gets. A chick is walking by who looks kind of cute in one of those period bathing suits. And that was all. So you know he's living there. But I'm taking them way down with Masha's suicide, which is certainly one of the great scenes in anything I've ever done. I can't look at it. And then you see the cemetery, very bare, very austere. I decided, finally, that the only way to give completion to this was to show the birth of the child. We're feeling better—at least Yadwiga had a baby— but we're not sure where we're going. Then we see the letter, and the twenty dollars, and the baby's named Masha. And I go for the music, which is good, and to the Coney Island Ferris wheel, and that's the movie. Well, it worked. I'll never forget the first time I showed it. I showed it in a room with eight or nine people. Roger had never seen it. He gasped. It was very moving. And the studio, Joe Roth and all those guys, said, "It's a masterpiece. Don't touch it."

And then we screened it for a test audience and it got the lowest marks in the history of marks. Like 35, beneath contempt.

Where did you screen it?

At Twentieth Century-Fox for two hundred people.

A focus group?

A focus group.

Aagh.

Two hundred people and I got a 35. So I said to Joe, "I'm giving up show business. The best thing for me to do is get out of the business." I said, "Joe, I'm not capable of changing this movie." He said, "I don't want you to. I don't want any changes. What this means, Paul, is that 35 percent of the audiences out there want to see this movie. We don't need more than 35 percent of millions of people out there to see this movie. It's a dark movie. I'm happy with 35 percent. Don't change a frame. I'm happy with it. We need reviews—we'll get 'em." And that's what happened. In later years, my dealings with the same Joe Roth—who I still like, by the way, he's a nice man—he turned me down on so many things, I can't even figure it out. But he's very proud of that movie, and Jim Robinson[48]—that's their claim to art.

I'm interested more in the writing process than in how you realized the writing. Who did the breakdown?

First we talked a lot. Then we had copies of the book which we put pencil marks around. I would say that I was more in "charge" of that in that I would suggest deep cuts from the book—we can't show this, we can't show that—and our collaboration was wonderful. Roger really wrote the first draft. There's no two ways about it. My biggest contribution was cutting. The dialogue is mostly right out of the book, and the changes we made in the dialogue were when we felt it was difficult to say.

One of the big dilemmas in making the movie was that, when you have accents in movies, if they're not alike, it blows it. You have a situation where you have a British person speaking this way (does British), somebody else is talking this way (Yiddish). I was trying to find a uniformity, and I decided to go with Yiddish accents. It's tricky because there's a few times in the movie where it's hard to understand, but that was my choice, and I would say it worked, for the most part, because I wanted you to feel their alien-ness in the United States, their being outsiders closed off from the American Yankee Doodle Dandy. The rabbi (Alan King) is the link—"Come on, I know lots of survivors—they have telephones, they go to the movies." And it's all in Singer. Singer did it all.

Speaking of the rabbi, at his party when Herman is publicly exposed as having three wives, Singer has him barfing into a handkerchief But you play it off-camera—

---

48 Joe Roth and James G. Robinson began Morgan Creek Entertainment in 1988 (named after Preston Sturges' *The Miracle of Morgan's Creek*) and released through Twentieth Century-Fox.

— I have him run for the bathroom—

So you can play it for the comic scene that it is, rather than distract the audience with seeing him be sick.

But you have to add to it that it's probably the best-cast movie I ever made. There's no mistakes. From Lena Olin and Ron Silver—I originally had Dreyfuss.

Yes, he was announced first.

And he wouldn't do it unless he could see the dailies with me, and I refused. So I got Ron. I went to see him in a play in New York written by David Mamet and I loved him and I said it's yours if you want to do it and he said yes. And that was it, and Joe Roth went with it. Margaret Stein (Yadwiga) I found through [director] Agnieszka Holland. I went to New York and I read her and gave her the part; she had to wait a year 'cause I didn't get the money for a year. Anjelica Huston I saw her very early on and we met in my other office twice, and that was it. It's one of her great performances. She is sweet, and it's a great performance. Maurice Jarre—a home run.

That's someone I want to talk about. Some parts of the score sound klezmerish and others are symphonic.

The score Maurice did for *Enemies* was fabulous. He has balls. You know, he's French-Jewish. I gave him a movie with klezmer music and he said, when he saw the movie, "I can't do better than that music, but let me take klezmer and enhance it give you thematic moments using the klezmer tone." Which he did. He gave it a theme for Herman and for each wife. Simple cord changes so you knew it was Masha, whoever it was. I can't tell you how much I think of him.

I was drawing some comparisons between Herman Broder (the Ron Silver character) and Steven Blume (George Segal in Blume in Love). *A kind of an arrogance in doing what he does.*

I can't see it. I don't see it. Critics might. Steven Blume is more of a precursor of a Yuppie, and Herman Broder is not a Yuppie. Herman is a guy who cannot find joy. The closest he comes to joy is an orgasm and some good prunes. He eats good, he likes to eat, and he likes to fuck. There's no joy in his life. He's seen the unbearable misery of those deaths, he knows his two children are dead. I always say that the scene where she goes off to the synagogue for Yom Kippur and he doesn't go, he's slapped her in the face and sent her out, and he's in the room alone, I shoot it like he's davening, which he basically was. And then he takes the pictures [of his dead children] out and looks at the pictures. Well, every time I see it, I start to cry. Every time. I can't handle it. Maurice's music, Ron's performance, and the faces of the two kids. And the next cut he's walking on the boardwalk, that beautiful shot, Fred Murphy the cameraman. Blume, no, Blume is much more of a—I think if Herman's wife kicked him out, he wouldn't worry about going back.

What's interesting, though, is he uses women without—

He gives in. That's it. When Masha says, "You gotta marry me" and goes crazy, he marries her.

Commitment is a big thing for someone who's had everything taken away.

So when he leaves at the end, don't be so surprised. He can't do it. She says, "I want to lay next to my mother." That's probably the most daring scene in the movie, the scene were she comes back in the taxi and her mother's dead, and she says, "I have nothing. I don't even have money for the funeral."

He says, "I bought a bulb." He screws the light bulb in. It's barely lit. And I play it with hardly any camera movement.

Finally she says, "Herman, you promised me once that if, blah blah, we'd kill ourselves." And I play the scene as a comedy.

"I promised you that?"

She says, "Yes you did."

And he thinks about it for a long time and finally says, "Okay, but first. . ." and she goes and lights a cigarette, and he asks, "Tell me, did you fuck Torchiner? Tell the truth."

She's laughing. Apparently it's funny. And she says, "Yeah, so what?"

"Then I'm not killing myself!"

"But you promised me! You promised me!"

And out of that turns this wonderful moment when he decides to leave, and she can go with him, and she goes in and combs her hair and looks at herself and she comes back out and she says, "I want to be buried next to my mother" and she forces him to go. And that moment when she holds him and says, "Goodbye, Herman," that's the best acting I've ever seen. Eye-yi-yi! Anyway, don't forget, Herman's biggest guilt is that he wasn't in the camps.

He was in a hayloft having his shit carried away by Yadwiga.

Right. That was daring: I wrote the scene in the hayloft so you see it, you don't imagine it.

I'd like to talk about some of the cuts that got you from script to screen. For example, when the rabbi (Alan King) goes on about why Herman doesn't have a telephone, he says, "A telephone isn't a Nazi. It doesn't eat people. You have a neurosis, go see a doctor." He goes on and on in the script, but in the film you cut after, "Hundreds of concentration camp survivors have telephones."

To be honest with you, I don't really remember whether I cut it in post or when I shot it. I might have cut it before I shot it. I had a reading—I don't have readings of every movie—but I did have a reading of this, and you get a sense of what's a little long. Some places I gambled and I'm glad I did. For example, there's a fairly long, talky scene around the table in the scene before

Herman fucks Masha for the first time. You see Masha and him kissing, the numbers on her arm, the first time we meet her, and they have the scene around the table with the mother and the cooking and the arguing, and there's a lot of talk about Is there a God, and "Mmm, these are the best prunes." It's a very Singer-ish, profoundly philosophical scene, about the meaning of life, about Herman and Singer's attitude, which basically is—I'm not a Singer scholar but I think I understand this—"this is the best we've got. It may not be perfect but I'd rather have this than nothing." He's filled with irony; it's what makes him so great. He never cops out. He's also very funny. Then you have the wonderful stuff with Herman calling Yadwiga on the phone and pretending that he's in the zoo, and Masha makes sounds, and later there's a critical argument when Yadwiga's had enough, and she says, "There is no zoo in Philadelphia." And the ghost scene[49] is staged very well, but that's Singer. The thing is, I never play them less than real.

And it works for her character.

She's a simple-minded peasant girl who believes it. And played with such intensity. And some of the great lines in it: Tamara, when she goes shopping with him, and says, "How do you manage to keep all these wives?" and he says, "It's not easy." It got a huge laugh.

When you find you have to trim a scene in post, do you have to scrounge around for a cutaway to cover the deletion?

I'm fairly good about that for two reasons. I have no fear of cutting myself out, and, secondly, when I shot it, I've thought about cutaways, and they're really not cutaways, they're ways of getting from a two-shot to a single and then back to the two-shot or back to another single where I'm just taking out eight lines. I did it in *Bob & Carol*, my first picture, many times. It's too fuckin' long.

---

49 Tamara walks in on Herman and Yadwiga and Yadwiga, thinking Tamara died in the camps, panics at seeing her ghost.

And you block it so you can pull it together?

You can do it if you've got coverage.[50] See, if I have coverage of the scene of me talking and you listening, and I say, "It's not like Steven Blume," and I cut to you nodding your head in agreement, and I cut back to me and I start talking about Alan King, it'll work. Physically it's gonna work. You don't want to jar them physically. That's what cutting is mostly about. The truth of the matter is, most audiences, including my wife, who is more sophisticated than not, never notice bad cutting in movies. I notice it right away; she'll never say, "Look at that jump-cut."

But if I'd crossed the room while talking about Steven Blume, then you'd be in a bind.

I might be, but even then, John Ford used to say, "Make a noise." Have a siren go by to distract them. I mean it.

Did they teach you that about cutting when you took courses at USC?

They didn't really. The only thing I ever studied at USC was editing. I read Karel Reisz's book and I took one year of editing, just me and Garry Marshall and a couple of other people. Later it became instructive.

There's one line in Enemies *that I want to ask you about changing. They're in the Catskills listening to a recording by Billie Holliday and the script has Masha say, "That schvartzer sure can sing." The movie says, "That girl sure can sing." At what point did you change that, and why?*

She doesn't say it in the movie? I probably did it right then and there. [The audience] probably wouldn't understand what sch-

---

50 "Coverage" is several different angles on the same scene that allow the editor and director numerous choices of how to construct the sequence of shots

vartzer means.⁵¹ Secondly, it's racist, and even though Jews, today, say it a lot, I didn't need it.

When you are writing a period piece such as Next Stop or Enemies, do you ever think to yourself, "If I put this scene in, it's going to cost a fortune to shoot"?

You don't think about it when you're writing. The best thing is just to write it. In *Enemies* there's great scenes in Coney Island in the late 40s, early 50s. I made that movie in 1990. It was out of the question for me to re-create Coney Island; I would need a million extras to depict a crowded day at the beach, and the parachute jump no longer works. You see the movie, the parachute jump works. I changed things, created things with the art director, Pato Guzman. We made it look like the parachute jump was still there and worked. We created the streets. Between the camera, Pato, and myself, and the costumer Albert Wolsky, we made a world. But I still was not satisfied with Coney Island. My editor said, "I know a guy at Universal who's in charge of all that stuff. Let me ask him for some of the old footage." So the guy comes back to me a week later and says, "Well, there was a movie made with Lana Turner, a color movie, and there are a couple of stock shots of Coney Island, I don't know if anybody ever used them." We put it in the movie and you look at it, and it's beyond belief! People ask, "How did you do that?" and I say, [feigns confidentiality], "That was the toughest thing. That's where most of the budget went. I used 2,000 extras." And I lie my brains out. It's stock footage that I matched into a scene!

Enemies *was highly praised, but your next film,* Scenes from a Mall, *was not appreciated, at least here in America.*

They liked it in Europe, they didn't like it here. You never know what's going to work. I know that they played it in France not long ago when I was there and they really like it. They get this farcical

---

51 *Schvartzer* is bastardized Yiddish for the German *schwartz*, meaning black. In practice, it's a derogatory term for an African-American.

crazy element of tragedy. See, as we were writing the script, I'm thinking of Kevin Kline and Meryl Streep. I get a call from Sam Cohn that Eisner called him 'cause Eisner heard that Woody was looking for a movie, and Sam says Woody is looking for a payday.[52] I said, "I don't know. Woody, he's got to play this real guy, and he's always Woody. Meryl, I don't know, Woody can't do it with Meryl." Then I get a call from Eisner himself. Reunite Bette who'd worked with me, and try to get Woody. I go through the whole thing in my head and it's an almost irresistible thing to work with those two people. So I sent the script to Woody Allen and in less than a day he says yes. Bette says yes. I'm off and running, but the tone of my picture has changed. It was a more serious—funny, but slightly more serious—exploration. I wanted it to be funny.

Sometimes you can be surprised at something that audiences find is funny that you didn't think was funny, and vice-versa.

That happens a lot. *Scenes from a Mall* is one of my favorite movies, but when the movie turned dark, we lost the audience. They did not want to see Woody in a serous, dark story. They wanted the old Woody.

They're not happy with him when he's that way in his own films, either.

They hate him—and this moron, Paul Mazursky, put him up to it. But up to the middle of the movie, the audience was on the floor. You couldn't hear at the test screenings: Woody and Bette in bed getting their separate phone calls, it all worked. Then he finds out that she's had an affair, and the whole audience turned the other way.

Woody brings a lot of baggage.

---

52 Hollywood slang for "doing it for the money." The film has a sports lawyer (Allen) and a shrink (Midler) hashing out their empty marriage in an equally jejune shopping mall.

I think his audience has trouble accepting him as anything but Woody. They want him to be "that guy." The film is a very heavy idea: a double confession in the confessional of the 21st century, the mall. The mall is where we go now for everything. We go to the mall to find sex, we go to the mall to find food, we go to the mall to see human beings, to shop, to see movies. To me I will be eternally grateful that somebody let me make a movie where two people have sex while that Indian film [Salaam, Bombay] is running. You know what I mean? With two people in the audience. The fact that they let me do that, I can go the rest of my life and be happy.

I had seen the film when it was new, and then again on video, and was surprised at how much I'd missed. It's also beautifully designed.

That's all Pato. I also had one of the great Steadicam operators. The movie was constructed in the following way. Woody wouldn't do it in California, which added a couple million to the cost. So I found a mall in Connecticut and we shot that for the big shots. Everything to do with the floor where all the action takes place, I built in a studio in New York. It's all built. The exterior is the Beverly Center. I got Woody to come out for two days to be in the car with Bette. He said, "I don't have a license."

You weren't dragging them in a camera car?

No. Bette was terrified that he had to drive.

Is it my imagination, or do the colors get brighter as the emotions in the film get higher?

We go into a bright Mexican restaurant. And by the way, the Mexican restaurant is where the movie turns. They're slightly loaded, and it's where she begins to find some kind of, something. That's when Eisner said to me, after he saw the preview, "I started to feel an itch in my pants." Something like that. Restlessness.

What he was saying, in essence, without him knowing that he was saying it—and he's very honest, a very good executive, there's no two ways about it. He's straightforward, that's why he's so accomplished. He tells you what's going on—he was sort of saying, "I don't know if the audience can handle this movie after it gets that route." It's got a wonderful sadness to it, a European sadness, I guess is the way to say it, when they look in at the dancers through the restaurant window, and then at the end they're back together, and you know they've been through something very heavy. That movie was a big disappointment to me that it wasn't very successful, and that it was financially a flop in the United States.

It's a very mature work. I don't mean old.

I know what you mean. I thought they did very well. Even Woody touched me. And in the early parts, of course, they were hilarious, so the audience thought it was all gonna be Woody and Bette in bed getting phone calls and all of that wonderful, crazy stuff.

Seeing Woody Allen in a pony tail carrying a surf board is a culture clash.

It's already hilarious. He didn't want to wear a pony tail, but he did everything for me, everything I wanted him to do. Take a look at that picture there [indicates a framed color 8x10 on his end table].

It says (reading), "To Paul, Pretty embarrassing when the director is funnier than the star. Woody Allen."

How's that! He meant it. He really did. Very affectionate. He's super-bright and all that, but as an actor he's rather limited. He does a lot of fumferring, which kind of works sometimes for him in his parts, but in real life it becomes the same guy over again.

Did you write the fumferring and stammering?

That's the way he does it. He's a masterpiece director. The guy's done ten great movies. The guy's only problem—I say, Woody—is that he's probably done too many pictures.

There's a lot of Preston Sturges in the film. One line from, I think, The Palm Beach Story, comes to mind, when Claudette Colbert says, "When love is gone from a marriage, all that's left is mutual respect." I think your film exemplifies that.

I wrote it with Roger Simon and we had a wonderful time. Roger is very fast. We would plot it out. We had just done *Enemies, A Love Story* and were exhausted from the Holocaust and a man with three wives. I think I came up with the notion but Roger was there, too, and I guarantee it, of two people in a mall and everything takes place there, with two confessions. That was our idea, and we wrote it by pitching back and forth in a room, doing scenes, and he would write it out, and we would pitch again and polish. We were happy with it; it got made very quickly when Disney came forth with the money. It looked like a sure-fire, commercial thing.

There's a mime in the film, Bill Irwin. Why do people like mimes?

All I know is that most of the malls I have been to, there's a mime. Down at Venice Beach they follow you, they walk like you. Some of them are good. That's all. And it's a tradition in Europe. People like it. He was an angry mime!

This is the film that carries the dedication "for Pato."

Yes, he died soon after. Pato Guzman.

The Pickle is a companion piece to Alex in Wonderland. Did you feel as creatively compromised at that point as Danny Aiello's character does?[53]

---

53 A once-successful personal filmmaker agrees to make a teen exploitation film strictly for the money, then suffers over "selling out" when he returns to his New

I really wanted to play the part myself. So we start with the dilemma—and it's not Danny's fault, because Danny is a very good actor. Michael Caine read it, and Michael Caine has irony galore. He's fabulous. And Michael Caine said to me (doing Caine), "I'd love to do it. Can you switch it to London. He's a Brit. I'll do it." I didn't do it. To me, New York's my town, Brooklyn's my town. Memories. It's all Americana. I didn't do it. I then went to Frank Price and said, "Let me play the guy. I can do it. I'll do it free." So my own sensibility is in there a lot, so it's a hard question for me to answer. It's not a question of compromise. In the movies that I have made, all of them, no studio ever forced me to compromise. Ever. Anything that's in there that you can say, Jesus, why was he soft? That's my doing. They never did it, even in post. The only trouble I ever had in post was *Faithful* (q.v.), but the movie that came out was my movie. No, I didn't feel compromised. I felt elated that I had a chance to make a movie about a guy who was making a movie about a flying cucumber. That's why Frank Price is an idol of mine. I went to him with *Tempest*, a movie about a guy who is making a storm; I went to him with *Moscow on the Hudson* which starts with 20 minutes in the Russian language; and then I went to him with *The Pickle*. So Frank, wherever you are, thank you.[54]

There's a special genre of explicitly autobiographical films. How do you feel about putting your life in front of strangers?

The way I look at it, *explicit* is the word that's probably important here. All of my films have autobiography in them, only because they reflect my views and my feelings and there's bits of me in it. But the only ones that are explicitly autobiographical are *Alex in*

York roots for the premiere.

54 Frank Price wrote for television before heading production at Columbia, then Universal, then back to Columbia. Despite his achievements as an outstanding executive, however, he may be remembered as the man who greenlighted *Howard the Duck* (1986) whose expensive failure caused his departure from Universal Pictures and was headlined in *Variety* with "'Duck' Cooks Price's Goose."

Wonderland, Next Stop, Greenwich Village, and *The Pickle*. Nothing else is explicitly autobiographical.

You've gone from being a writer-director of whom it's often said that you love your characters to The Pickle where there's not a lot of affection for them. Barry Miller's studio head, the agent Hirsch—there's always something that mitigates against our having real affection for them. It's cynical for you.

I can't really examine my own films, but I'm trying to think about that. The Barry Miller guy, I think, is so amusing that I have affection for him.

Maybe because I've had to deal with jerks like that, I find his stupidity malicious.

But he's funny to me. I don't have affection for the studio people. There's no question about it. And I make fun of them at that wonderful scene around the table. I do have affection for the Jerry Stiller character, Danny's long-time agent/manager. And Shelley Winters, the mother—there's an odd affection. And for the grandchild. The movie was saying that the projectionist, who is played by the director *of* the movie [Mazursky], calls the director *in* the movie, who is killing himself, and says, "They love it." I never examined the Freudian meaning of all that stuff, but there's affection there. Certainly the character I play has affection for him. There's even affection for his crazy mother, which I've done before with Shelley, when you see her as a young woman playing opera, which I used in *Next Stop, Greenwich Village,* and I used it again here.

Arguably, Harry Stone [Aiello's character] does, in fact, commit suicide at the end.

He doesn't, though. He's saved.

Well, if you take it from the point of view of the device that Ambrose Bierce used in An Occurrence at Owl Creek Bridge, *he's fantasizing his reprieve and success just before he dies.*

The way I see it, the utter irony is that he's prepared to kill himself—and he really means it because he's made a piece of shit to make money—and when he's told that the piece of shit is gonna be a hit because the audience loves it, he not only runs out of the hotel with a certain kind of joy, but he's on his way to pitching his next movie, which is about his son. He's back to work. Movie directors are like that. We constantly die and are reborn. It's a very tricky movie which, again, was sold like death. They didn't like it, and when they don't like a movie—first of all, they didn't show it to the critics in time for the Friday reviews. A critic named Michael Wilmington called me and told me this was happening. I called the publicist who was working on the picture and confronted her and she knew about it and I said, "This is the end. How dare any of you?" I then called Sid Ganis[55] and said, "How could you guys do this to me? If a movie made by me is not shown to the critics, it's a death knell." "Well, we wanted it to open good."

That's an admission.

To begin with, it's a small movie with Danny Aiello, it's not a big movie with John Travolta or kickboxing. It's not gonna open strong anyway. "It *needs* reviews; what's *wrong* with you?" You do what you always used to do in the past: you find a rabbi. That's what they used to do with tough movies.

Find a "rabbi"?

You find a critic who will champion it. A rabbi. When I see reviews in the paper on Friday for a picture that's opening, unless it's the four or five critics that we all know, I disregard it entirely. There's no meaning to reading the reviews. They mention papers where it's flacks.

---

55 Studio advertising-marketing executive

How difficult was it to make a film-within-the-film that's supposed to be a bad movie, but have it look like it still has potential?

That's very tricky. I tried to make something absurd. I must say, I was very touched by the fact that Griffin Dunne, Isabella Rosselini, and Ally Sheedy helped me. They knew this was a send-up and a lark, and they did it. I had a crazy thing where people were wearing Spandex. I'd never done special effects. We had wonderful production designer in Jim Bissell, a brilliant man, and I had a great time making it, knowing I had this dilemma of wanting the kind of irony you get from Jack Nicholson. You know, for something to work 100 percent, it's almost like a miracle. If you make a movie and it really works—even if let's say 90 percent—it's a miracle. You cast Dyan Cannon, Natalie Wood, Elliott Gould, Bob Culp, an unknown guy directs it from a script by two people nobody ever really heard of, and everything falls into place. It seems that simple. And then you have the ones where it's a struggle and conflict and craziness and nothing falls into place, and yet, when you see it, it looks like it did. And then you have the third category, which is most movies: they don't work.

Let's go to Faithful, which is a three-hander and very cleverly directed. But this is the first film you've directed that you didn't write.

Well, *Faithful* was written by Chazz Palminteri. It had been a play and Chazz had played the part of the hit man. This was after *The Pickle* and I was sitting around doing my usual: trying to get *Pictures of Fidelman* made, and one or two others you now know about. One of them was called *Nirvana* and that's back out in the field as we speak, so we'll see. But I got a call about *Faithful*, so I read it, and I liked it. I always try to go by my first reaction to anything. I met with Bob DeNiro (producer) and Chazz Palminteri and Frank Price and I made it. We cast Cher and had a delightful shoot. Dark comedy, almost all in the house, Fred Murphy camera. Lots of problems due to long shots and this and the other. Ryan O'Neal, we took a big chance; nobody would hire him. I played the psychiatrist, the part that they later made a whole movie out of [Analyze This] with Billy Crystal and Bob DeNiro. It's all stolen from this movie, every bit of it.

That didn't even occur to me.

Of course. I liked [Faithful], and I found out when I finished cutting it that Cher saw it and Bob saw it and they *didn't* like it. Chazz seemed to have liked it, but Bob's his pal and then he didn't, and they let Cher re-cut it. I can't tell you the rest because it's all worked out, it's just not cricket [but] it all worked out and my cut is the one that you saw.

You had threatened to take your name off it, to do an Alan Smithee.

I went to a lot of trouble and it was unfortunate and it left a bad taste. I didn't do anything wrong, but I'm very sorry it happened because once the word gets out that a film is going through something like that, it's pretty much dead in this business. So who'll ever know. I don't want to go into it because it's not pleasant. Whatever it was, it seemed ridiculous.

Cher doesn't always have a lot of confidence in her work, and she should.

She's very good. She's breathtakingly touching. But somewhere along the line she lost confidence in it and she swears it's not because of the way she looks—she wrote in a letter to me "even though I look a hundred years old." And that's the way it is. She's very gifted. I think if someone sees the movie—look, they showed the movie at the Berlin Film Festival. I was there before it opened in New York. I've been to a lot of my films' screenings. If they don't like it, you get a reaction that they don't like it. They really liked it. What can I tell you? I'm sitting there in Berlin with this largely German audience enjoying this movie. I don't know what to say.

She wanted to change the music, she wanted to change a lot of stuff. Oh, God, you don't want to hear about it.

Did you have input in the script but not take credit for it?

No. The script is all Chazz Palminteri's. If I would change a line or a word, Chazz was there, and I would say to him that I think you ought to do X or Y. My big job in directing the picture, in a way, was that this guy had already played the part on stage, and I, at times, wanted certain other elements from it.

Was he protective of his words?

He didn't seem to be crazy at all. We had a great time, I'm trying to tell you. We had great rehearsals, very inventive stuff, I was very inventive in staging it. One of the things I did in this movie was that I went with the art director/production designer, Jeff Townsend, and we got a little video camera and I staged most of the movie in the house on video with Jeff, myself and a couple of ADs and assistants, just walking the physicality of the parts. I had them up on the stairs, down here, over here, I did cuts, I prepared it.

As you did on Down & Out.

But more, even more, because I was afraid, because of the confinement, of it being boring. But in my mind it was anything but boring, and some people really got that and some didn't.

After Faithful, you made Winchell, another script you had not written. It was produced for HBO. How did that go?

It's a very good script. Scott Abbott is a wonderful young man who wouldn't come to the set, the opposite of what the Writers Guild was always asking for. I would call him up and say, "Scott, in scene *this* on page *that*, instead of 'Tell me, Walter, do you have anything in you to do this?' we're going to say, 'Walter, would you do this for me?'" I would just tell him the smallest changes because

I respect the writer, and he's a wonderful young guy. I got to a point in the scene with Stanley Tucci—who is a great American actor and no trouble in a big, tough part—in a hotel room scene with Glenne Headly, a tough scene, and Stanley says to me—it's nine-thirty in the morning and we've lit the scene and we're rehearsing—"I can't do it. I can't do it. It's no good. It doesn't work." He gives me the reasons. You can feel the heart pounding 'cause it's HBO and you've really got to go. I think, "Wow, we've really got to go," and I say, "Could everybody leave us?" I sit there with him and Glenne and say, "Tell me in your own words what's bothering you and what you think might be wrong. And we go 'round and some assistant is writing it down. I take a half hour and have it typed up, and I take the scene we had, but I make some 15 percent changes, 20 percent maybe. They read it and he says, "The scene works." It's an hour and a half later—it's now 11 o'clock—and I call Scott Abbott, tell him I changed the scene. He didn't give a shit. It was fine. In that case it worked. In other words, the actor was saying, "I can't act the scene. I can't make these emotional changes." And I think he was right. Even though they seemed small, they were critical. So you have to listen to the artist and you'd be a fool not to listen if they're really intelligent people. It's when it's about ego that it gets dangerous.

*You performed a miracle in **Winchell**, which was making us have sympathy for the swine.*

Winchell's a great script. This kid, Scott Abbott—I had never met him. I read it once and called my agent, said I wanted to do it. Just like that. They called me back, asked when can you meet, and it's a deal. Then we cast it and did it. The financial limitations—HBO is a wonderful place to work. When you say to HBO, "If I had another three or four days and another $400,000," they listen. And they gave it to me. I had 37 days and a week in New York. Without the week in New York I'd have nothing, the picture wouldn't work. Everything in this picture is made up. Everything. Because nothing is the same any more in New York. All the interiors were all shot here. The Hearst scenes were in some nunnery or something in downtown LA. I used the Paramount back lot for the streets of New York, when he gets hit by the horse as a kid. Robbie Greenberg, master. And a great cast. Some rehearsal. And we pulled it off. Got Bill Conti back to do the score.

The film was from Winchell's point of view for about half an hour, then it switches to Klurfeld's[56] point of view when his character is introduced and Winchell hires him.

It's based on Klurfeld's book; the producers paid for the rights. I later met Klurfeld several times, he's a kind of fun old guy—so it's told a lot from his point of view. Not the early stuff, but when he gets into it, he's telling it from his point of view. Which I accepted.

Changing the point of view works but I can't explain why.

It did on paper.

The Neal Gabler book[57] wasn't out at that time, was it?

I think it was. The Gabler book is brilliant and it's got more specificity. You know that Marty Scorsese was threatening to make a movie of this, based on the Gabler book, for a long time. But, I'll tell you something. HBO is brilliant at screening. We showed the movie in New York, and they assembled a brutally tough audience: Mike Wallace, Neal Gabler, lots of reporters were there. People who had known Winchell. I was scared. They liked it. I was relieved. They believed it.

There was also a project that Stirling Silliphant had started about Walter Winchell and Damon Runyon who had a very complex relationship.[58]

---

56 *Walter Winchell: His Life and Times* by Herman Klurfeld (NY: Praeger Publishers, 1976), who was Winchell's legman for many years.
57 *Winchell: Gossip, Power, and the Culture of Celebrity*, NY: Alfred A. Knopf, 1994
58 Reportedly, Runyon detested Winchell but Winchell, not knowing this, admired Runyon.

The way I look at is that when you do a story about a cad, if there's anything redeeming about him, great. It seemed to me that he was redeeming in a couple of very specific ways that seemed to be based on real truth. He had the courage to talk about the Jews with Roosevelt. That stuff works, and he did it. He went on the air and talked about the storm troopers and the Nazis and the Jews. It wasn't popular. Chris Plummer was great [as Roosevelt]. But Winchell was a cad. Terrible treatment of the wife, kids. No one came to the funeral except the daughter.

He's an interesting American study in that he was seduced by his own power, like Louella and Hedda were, too, and it's an interesting relic of a time when a self-made man with self-made issues can so grip the public.

That was an era when "the media" was the print press. And Walter Winchell was king. The script showed some nice touches just how strong he was. People would come to him for favors. His treatment of the woman (Headley), who was a combination of Texas Guinan and others, that's devastating treatment.

Glenne Headley was wonderful.

Yes, she was great. And he was hoist by his own petard quite savagely with all the McCarthy stuff.

It's also an important film in that it finally portrays Hearst as anti-Semitic. Which everybody knew but the public, apparently.

That was daring.

Did Winchell really jam it up Hearst's ass about Hitler?

Apparently he did. Hearst threatened to fire him, and Winchell said "fuck you, I don't care." Later, he did have trouble from him. Hearst was very powerful, but Winchell was not afraid. And the sad part about Winchell—which I thought we did very well in this movie—was that, at the end, he was reduced to doing a song-and-dance routine in Vegas.

A whole generation knows him only as the narrator of **The Untouchables** *TV series.*

But to do the song-and-dance in Vegas and do that little act, I thought that was good.

Tucci played that well in that he had to have the veneer of respectability, and at the same time, underneath, you saw that the man was crumbling, someone whom you're happy is crumbling, but still.

At the time of this conversation I may—I *may*—do something about Peter Sellers. He was not a good guy either. But if you tell the truth, somehow it seems to work.

People are interesting sometimes for their weaknesses, not their strengths.

Right.

THERE ARE NO RULES

Nat Segaloff: When you are writing, do you have set hours and force yourself to do X pages a day?

Paul Mazursky: My tendency has always been to write in the morning when I have the most energy. So I would get to my office at some point, I would say by 9:30 or 10, and write till about 1.

Straight through?

Sometimes nothing. One word. Sometimes seven pages. Very rarely. But I always like to leave knowing that, tomorrow when I come in, I'll start with X. I manage to do that about half the time. I'll have that next day's "thing" in my head. The trick is just to plow through it and then, after a first draft, to take a couple of days off, read it, and then go back and start again and then, at some point, show it to somebody to see if I'm out of my mind.

When you're writing and you leave something till the next day, do you then re-read everything you've written to get up to momentum?

I don't plan to, but I often do. I find myself going back two pages, then saying, "wait a second." Then I try to get a run at it. One of the other reasons for doing that is that you have 30 minutes less to write; you'll do *anything* to delay. You'll sharpen a pencil for 30 minutes. "I want to sharpen *all* my pencils. I don't want to sharpen one pencil. Not only that, the chair is so low somehow, and I can't find a screwdriver." Finally it's already noon. Thank God. I've done a lot of that, I really have. And, to be honest with you, I'm 71 years old, I feel very good, right now I have an idea that's tossing around in my head and I have another idea that's been tossing around. But I haven't committed to writing either one, really. When I say "committed" I mean this: for me, commitment means everything else is over. This is what I am going to do for the next three months. I'm gonna write. "I'm busy, I can't do that next week." "I can't do that for the next three months." My door is closed. I haven't done that in about a year. It may be over. I may have tapped out. I don't know. Because that commitment means that *you're gonna write something.*

It's an enormous expenditure of concentration and energy.

Not only that, but you're making a commitment and you're letting a certain group of people know it, And then, if nothing happens, *nothing*! Except my wife; she doesn't care. She has no expectations and never pushes; she's wonderful. But if I let the guys at the Farmer's Market know that I'm writing, they'll ask me, with a regularity that's deadening, "What's happening? How's the script? How many pages have you written? Is it any good? When will I see it? Are you gonna get it made?" They don't stop.

Do they understand what you have to go through?

They sort of do, but they're killers.

Do you get a physical sensation when you're writing and it's going well?

I haven't had it in so long that I don't know. You just feel it. You're just interested, I don't know, it involves you. The trouble is—and I know this from the scripts that I've written or the scripts that have been given me—most writers like what they've done. Very often there's not much agreement about it. I have as much admiration for the Epstein brothers' *Casablanca* as I would for *La*

Dolce Vita. In its own way it's a masterpiece of tongue in cheek entertainment. It's hard to write that stuff. When you put in lines—when you're as sophisticated as they were—like "My advice to you is to go back to Bulgaria." They've *got* to have known that's funny. But it worked for the time, and it still works. So when you come up with something that pleases you, it's a satisfactory feeling.

Do you say your lines out loud as you're writing them?

Sometimes I say the whole script out loud before I hand it in. By the time I reach a first draft, I've gone through it, talking it. One of the things that I have as a big advantage is that I'm an actor, so many of the roles I've played over the years, you can't say some of the words. It's impossible to physically say them without getting your tongue caught in your mouth. Obviously whoever wrote it didn't know you've got to say it. It might look good.

How, physically, has your writing changed? Did you start with pencil and paper, typewriter—

I used to work with a pad and a pencil and outline it. Then I used a typewriter. I typed 55 words a minute. Outlines, a lot of pencil, yellow pad, throw it away, tap out a step outline. In the case of *Bob & Carol*, Larry Tucker and I were trying to get money to write the script, so we wrote a 15-20 page outline. I have it somewhere. Very close to the movie. No one wanted to give us the money, they just wouldn't. And I realized it was because they thought it was too dirty—"two couples switching, what are these guys, crazy? Is this porno?"—so we knew we had to write it on spec, which we did. But getting back to your question, obviously I used to type the script, Xerox a couple of copies, go to the desert, and cut and paste using a scissors, Scotch tape and a typewriter. Start to rewrite, shape, throw out, all that stuff, which later the computer made obsolete. Roger Simon, whom I've written five scripts with, is a computer whiz, boom boom boom; me, I'm just not that fast. But when it comes to writing, a computer is a fabulous thing.

I've often wondered if having to change paper or erase, in the typewriter days, almost compelled a writer to think a scene through first instead of just dicking around on the computer.

I would like to think there's truth in it. The computer, like everything else, has made things go quicker. And the quicker things go, the less chance you'll take your time and think about it. Just to go to the trouble of using a scissors and Scotch tape—it was a nightmare, but you thought a lot about it. I would have hundreds of pieces of paper all over the floor, all over the desert, then I used to roll them up and throw them out and go and buy more paper. It's a pain in the ass. The computer saves you a lot of time and it does short-cut, but it might lead you to be too quick, too hasty. One of the problems with this business is that it's not just that you're only as good as your last picture, it's that they really don't care. It chews up stuff. If you stop and think about any of us who have been around for thirty or forty years, how many things can you do? Most people go fishing after writing and directing sixteen movies, but I can't do that.

When you're writing and you're not thinking about a particular actor you want to cast, are you thinking about such things as, "Does the character have a star entrance?" "What makes a role attractive to an actor?" and so forth?

I don't really think about that very much, when it's over and I've read it and acted it out, which I've done. Pato Guzman was a great pal to be able to talk about the script. So I made him co-producer, and for the last few movies we did, I'd have him around more, in order to talk about it. I'd act out every scene, not always good, but I'd do it, and in the course of doing that, you'd see, "Boy, this is really a juicy part, no one could possibly turn this down." But you never know what they want. I have a script which I wrote with Roger Simon which is an adaptation of a novel by Bernard Malamud called *Pictures of Fidelman*. It's mentioned in my book as one of the movies I couldn't get made. I've been trying to get it made for eight or nine years. The only actor who ever agreed to do it was Nic Cage, and he ended up not doing it because I couldn't get the money, and then when I *could* get the money, he wanted *more* money, and it didn't work out. I've been turned down by every pretty-good actor in the business. It's a great script. In my mind, it's a tremendous opportunity for a great performance. Turned down! You never know what they're looking for. Fidelman is a great role. He's a failed New York painter who goes to Italy to discover art and ends up, as Malamud has, having a series of episodic things happen over two or three years, which are funny, tragic, dark, ironic, interesting, and at the end he goes back to New York older and wiser. It's a wonderful part. Nobody was interested. If you asked me seven years ago if everyone would have turned this down, I would have said it's not possible.

You mean nobody the studio considered bankable wanted the part?

I went to guys like Liev Schreiber—they're not big stars—Adrian Brody, I pretty much had him, and then it didn't happen. All those middle-level talented names. I went to some of the bigger names. I think I went to Richard Dreyfuss when he was younger, and he didn't want to do it. You just don't know. And then you see them in scripts which are [winces] clearly not high-class material, but they might have been a payday.

When you're writing a scene, do you ever think about how you're going to direct it?

I don't think about it very much. Almost all my scripts have almost no stage directions. I don't write "Zoom in.." The only kind of stage directions that are needed are those that are very specific to try to tell the story. You want the reader to understand. There's two reasons people put in things. Most writers who haven't sold, or are afraid, or don't know, are going to overwrite directions because they presume the reader won't get it. So they say "Zoom in" badda-boom, budda-bom. I have dialogue and a setting—"Interior—Office—Four O'clock. The lights are on, pictures all over the walls, they're facing each other." That's it. Then there's dialogue. No shots.

What about the people who write all the books about screenwriting?

They don't know. They don't know. I'll get killed for this, but I'm against a lot of those books. There are no rules! Structure? Every movie you show me, I'll show you one that defies every one of those rules and it's s great movie.

Today authors like John Truby, Robert McKee, Linda Seeger and others have pretty much standardized how scripts are written. Worse, they've standardized how "Jason," the generic 25-year-old development executive, analyzes what's good and what's bad in other people's work.

They may have, but the results are so catastrophic that what's there to talk about?

But do scripts have to hit a certain reveal on page 30, must there be something that happens on page 66—

I don't worry about the other person's scripts. I'm not the least bit concerned. I only go by the movies I see. If the guy or woman who wrote the movie I saw did a great job, and they were helped or influenced by one of these people, fine. But most of the movies I see are not very good, so they couldn't've gotten much help if they were going to these people. There's nothing wrong with going to a teacher or a study—I'm not criticizing that—but years ago (it's a mark of the time) I used to read John Howard Lawson.[59] He was the guy we all read. Then John van Druten, the playwright, who wrote a wonderful book,[60] too, which said, among other things, that if, for two acts, you talk about a volcano that's going to erupt, you better show the volcano in the third act. You

---

59 *Film the Creative Process*, op. cit.
60 *Playwright at Work*, NY: Harper & Brothers, 1953

can't tease us and then not do it. I thought it was a good lesson. In other words, you want there to be something in the movie that the audience begins to build an expectation about happening so that you hold onto that. But what's happened is that we've sacrificed character to such a great degree now that we don't care what happens because they're not real, they're not dimensional, they're not human. Humph, maybe something will happen, maybe not. So it's got to be the energy of the events—the car chase, the murder.

Sometimes you get so swept along by the action of a film—Hitchcock was like this—that you just don't ask questions.

But Hitchcock had a couple of things going. He had an odd psychological density even though the pictures appear to be simple and the characters are, if anything, cardboardy at times. They're not method actor-type characters. But *Vertigo* is a masterpiece. It's so dense, so complicated emotionally. I don't even want to analyze Alfred Hitchcock.

Let's take the three tiers of Paul Mazursky now. How you regard script changes on your own films as writer, then when you get to the floor as director, then when you act in your own films?

If I'm acting in somebody else's movie, and I didn't write the script, I will not change it unless I'm asked. I respect whoever write it because whoever wrote it had reasons, I presume, for doing it. Same as for my films. A lot of people think my movies are improvised. They're not. There's almost none. It's written, but I'm very good with actors, so it looks like they're making it up. Writing is the toughest of all the things in many ways. I have no doubt about it. I don't want to get into the whole WGA/DGA conflict. But even though I have said that writing is the toughest thing because you're starting with the blank page, even if you're adapting a book, it's very hard but, once it's written, the writer must surrender to the director. That's the problem.

Let's get into that hand-off period. Presumably by the time you've budgeted the script and cast it, it's the script you want. But then you get to the table read and you're hearing other people speak it—

You've got to be prepared to be tough. If something's not working, change it. If it's *really* not working, cut it. I have no trouble doing that, although I'm the first to admit that, every movie I've made, I've ended up with several scenes that I've cut. I wish I'd known it before I shot the movie because I would have saved those days. But you don't know the whole until you finish. You just don't. You don't know about the pace until you see it with an audience, and then you say, "Jesus, this thing is taking forever" or "This is repetitious" or "they get it."

Paddy Chayefsky once said that drama comes about when you ask: who is your hero? What is his goal? Who stands between your hero and his goal? Given that, what structure do you have for drama?

It's a generalization, but I think I like to come up with a problem. It's combining two things: character and a problem. A real problem. The problem is not "should I eat corned beef or go on a diet?" The problem is deeper. In *Harry & Tonto* they tear down the building in which he'd lived for forty years, where his wife lived with him. He's there with his cat. Where is a man in his 70s going to live? He tries his son and daughter-in-law in Queens; that doesn't work. He goes to Chicago to see the daughter in Chicago, the divorced one. And he goes to California to see the son, who's living by himself. The plot is all laid out for you. The problem with this specific guy—"Where am I going to live?"—led to the plot. In *An Unmarried Woman* an apparently very happy marriage, a good marriage, a solid marriage, a very attractive couple, plenty of money, upper-middle class, a lovely, bright daughter, everything's great. And then he tells her at lunch, of all places, "I fell in love with somebody while I was buying a shirt at Bloomingdale's." And she throws up and the movie goes into act two, which is What do you do with your life when you no longer have a husband—when you're unmarried? That's the problem.

There's also the Stanislavsky improvisation where one character wants and the other won't give—.

I never think of stuff like that ever, ever, ever. In *Blume in Love*, a guy is caught having an affair, a one-time, crazy, stupid affair with his secretary and his wife kicks him out, and he finds himself more in love than ever—*with the wife*. That's the movie. All the rest is an invention. I don't like rules too much. I'm nervous about them. I find that rules tend to make people think that, if they're obeying them, they're writing good.

That's what I brought up about Truby and Field and Seeger.

It all depends on what you're doing. If the character's interesting there's lots of room for other things. It's great to have a "what's gonna happen" thing at some point early in the script. If you don't have any of that—and life and death make it easier. That's why there are so many bad movies. The guy's in danger and they're chasing him, or they're gonna blow him up, so he dives through the window with the fire behind him. That's in every movie that comes out now. Fake life and death. *Real* life and death movies, like *Enemies, A Love Story*, which is about a man who ends up with three wives—one of them threatens suicide and finally commits suicide, the other one finds out that he's been cheating with a mistress, and the wife who's supposedly dead comes back alive and is the one who gives him solace and even goes to bed with him again. It's a brilliant plot, and dealt with realistically, not sketch-wise.

There's a syndrome I hear about in which you've been writing a script and rehearsing it for two years, then you get to the floor and somebody thinks of another line which sounds better than anything you have, and it really isn't, it's just that you've become bored with the script and anything new sounds better.

I haven't had that happen. I have not been a victim of what I'm about to say, but I know it's out there. It could happen to me, but it really hasn't. And that's what I call the Movie Star Auteur who agrees to do your movie, and as time goes on begins to ask for rewrites, changes, script things—"my character would never do this"—whatever it would be. Then when you get there to shoot it [you get], "I can't do this scene." I've heard stories about stuff like that where you make changes because you want to get the fucking movie done. Changes that lean toward the taste of the star. Stars have a lot of power and they think they know what's good for *them*, but not necessarily for the *movie*. I've never really encountered that; I've had a wonderful journey in that sense. I was blessed. I was left alone by all these people for so many years: Natalie Wood and Art Carney and George Segal, Anjelica Huston, Lena Olin, Richard Dreyfuss, Bette Midler, Nick Nolte, Robin Williams. No trouble. Discussions, some arguments, some tension, some disagreement, but not Trouble with a capital T.

Do you ever have a character just appear and take over a scene and you weren't expecting him?

That's a nice thing when that happens. It's like a reward. I didn't write *The Big Chill* (Barbara Benedek and Lawrence Kasdan, 1983), but they had a lot of characters. I never asked Larry, "did you write a history for each one? Did you know all of them before you started writing, or did they start to get clearer [as you went along], or were they based on eight people you knew?" I wonder. I usually try to base it on knowing someone like the person. Never an actor. I've never written saying, "This is a Jack Nicholson role," because he's an actor, he's not a human being. He is, but you know what I'm saying. You don't want to get stuck on an actor. Now, I *did* write *Alex in Wonderland* thinking that Elliott Gould would play Alex, but he didn't want to do it, and Donald Sutherland played the part. So when I wrote it, I did have him in my head. But most of the other times, I try to think of real people. Every now and then when you write a script somebody comes into the page and they take over, and you can't get them out. I generally try to go with that if I can, because it must mean something positive, but you don't know.

How has home video changed screen syntax?

People have less patience. They're quicker to say, "Oh, I know, the guy's gonna do X." So you may not need as much time to tell certain stories. But I must say that, when you see an old picture and it works, you like it. You like the time that they took to show you the character. I saw, for example, a few weeks ago, *Anatomy of a Murder*. If I was grading it, I would give it a nice "B." Solid, entertaining. Otto Preminger takes his time. Builds you Jimmy Stewart's guy, he's fishing and cleaning his reels; Arthur O'Connell the drunken lawyer who comes to him; Eve Arden the secretary; Ben Gazzara the bad guy, and Lee Remmick the sexpot who probably lured the guy on to rape her; I was involved. It even had a good ending. That movie, today, would have to be much jazzier. *And I don't think it would have worked*. It was all left to your imagination: she had a sweater ripped with a high bra. Today she'd be nude.

When young writers use the term "Smash Cut to," what the hell does that mean?

A smash cut is an attempt on the part of the young writer to make the reader feel that there's going to be so much energy that the audience will jump out of their seats. It's an excuse for good writing. "Smash cut" means, in their minds, that the cut will be so fast and so sudden that it will have the effect of a smash. It won't be a gentle cut where I cut gently from us in this room to a water cooler where somebody's getting a cup of water. It would be a cut from us in this room to a water cooler being cracked open with an axe. Smash. I don't like to read scripts like that. It alienates me, almost always.

Now they're even taking out transitions like "continued and "cut to." Everything's written in masters.

That's okay. Have you ever read a Bergman script? It reads like a short story. Plus, he doesn't have to sell it to a studio executive who can't read. It's easier for the executive to read, "Exterior: the dinosaur pounds on his head brutally. Dialogue: Bill: "Look" Jack: "What?" Bill: "There!" "Oh my" "Yes" "It's Dino!" "Oh!" Cut to: Dino's big giant foot smashes the car and head of so-and-so. Cut: blood rushing from so-and-so's eye and ear. Cut: Blood trickling on ground. Cut: Wide shot, Jurassic Park."

When your script goes into the studio process do you write two different versions: a reading script for the executives, and a shooting script for the filmmakers?

I've never done anything like that. The other thing I've never done is that I've never been paranoid about showing a finished script. Woody Allen won't do it. Most of the actors who are in Woody Allen movies don't see a script, they only see their scenes. For example, the location manager on Woody's movies, who has done several of mine, told me that when he did *Interiors*, which was shot in the Hamptons, Woody wouldn't show him a script. So he said, "How am I going to find you a location?" and Woody said, "I want a house in the Hamptons near the beach." That's all he told him. I have never been paranoid. I realize that once you give it in, it's going to be photocopied and every agent in town is going to get it and it's going to be stolen. In the case of *An Unmarried Woman* there was even a television series where there was an unmarried woman who had a job in an art gallery before the fucking movie came out! How did that happen? Was that a coincidence. Nah. Outright steal. I don't worry about it.

So you don't worry about studio notes?

Again, I haven't suffered the slings and arrows of outrageous notes. Don't forget, I had a period of enormous power. I don't have it now. But if I had all those notes now, I wouldn't do the picture. For example, when I did *Down and Out in Beverly Hills*, at Touchstone Pictures, I gave the script to Jeffrey Katzenberg and Michael Eisner. I went in and we had one meeting where they had four notes, and they were not written down. And you listen. Sometimes they're sensible and they work. But I hear stories now! It's unbelievable. They get 25 pages of notes.

That raises the age-old question, if they like a script enough to buy it, why don't they shoot it?

You're dealing with a combination of things that have to do with the studio executive being a meaningless person if he doesn't contribute, and he contributes by giving notes. Leon [Capetanos] tells me nightmare stories. We're doing something now—we've just finished a script for Showtime—where we had one set of notes, and I thought they were very good, not major, and we've handed that version in. And they apparently like it, but we're apparently getting more notes a week from Monday. By my next interview, when I know what those notes are, I'll let you know if I'm doing it. Because I know that after one series of notes, if the second set starts to get crazy—such as "on page 76 do they have to say 'would you'"—then I'm not gonna do it. But all those years I didn't have that. They were afraid. They'd think, "I'm not gonna tell the guy that made *Bob & Carol & Ted & Alice* what to do." If you don't make a picture that's a hit, they're not afraid. You know, with *Bob & Carol*, the first guy we went to with the idea to get money for it was National General [a now-defunct studio of the late 1960s and early 1970s]. The guy who read the 20-page treatment—all we were looking for was 50 G's at that time, it was 1969—said, "This is dirty. We can't make this." So I said, "Well, if I get Paul Newman and Joanne Woodward for one couple," and he said, "Well, then it wouldn't be dirty." That's when I told Larry Tucker, "Larry, we better write the whole script, because somebody's either gonna do it or not." And Larry was a great guy so he said yes.

When they tell you "it's all in the execution," it means—

—They haven't got a clue.

NO TRICKS IN MY POCKET

Nat Segaloff: How does it help you as a director having been an actor?

Paul Mazursky: I don't think I could direct without having been an actor. I don't start out thinking visually about the camera. I think about the character: why, where, who, all those things I learned being an actor. And having been an actor I know buttons to press, I know when not to press, and I have ideas about how to work which sometimes are very helpful, which are deceptively simple if done right, but they can really help an actor out of trouble. For example, let me give you one that's not new or original: you find an activity for the actor to do that has nothing to do with the dialogue. So if the scene is you and me interviewing, and I'm going to shoot this scene, but I'm putting up one of my awards during the course of the entire interview—I'm getting up, I'm measuring the wall, I'm getting the frame, I'm motioning for you to help me at the same time—that takes me off the words. As an actor I'm not thinking about the words any more, I'm thinking about, "Where do I put this fuckin' nail?" That's something I learned early on and it's been useful. Often actors get hung up on the words and they act the words. THEY SPEAK THE WORDS AND DO THE WORDS! And, of course, Marlon was the guy who helped break the mold of all that because he'd be [does Brando while examining his fingernails] scratching, he's got a little dirt in his ear while he's saying, "you know, we're gonna have to kill you if you don't. . .we would probably use a knife, but we could use a gun. . ." and all that stuff. It helps actors. The second thing is that

I'm comfortable with rehearsing, so I like to rehearse. And the third thing is that I don't panic if the actor says, "I can't do it." I've been around movies and television that I've acted in where the actor was having trouble and the director had no idea of what to do except to say, "Give me more" or "a little less." Sometimes it works, but what do you do if you get into real trouble?

Do actors automatically trust you, knowing you've been where they've been?

Up to now they have, but I don't think this new generation knows who I am, so I doubt if they'll trust me. I'm meeting one at 2:30 for something that I'm involved with, and I don't think this kid has seen any movie I've ever made.

But aren't there vibes that actors send out to each other?

I think when an actor knows that you've directed a very successful movie, that's a good vibe. If he doesn't, he's scared.

All actors are scared.

Do they trust? I romanced Warren Beatty over a thirty year period and we never did anything. We just did a tango, but never completed the dance. I think the bigger the star, the less they trust most people. They feel that they know more, they know better what's right for them, they want to do a star turn, and you need an exceptional actor or actress to beat all that nonsense. I think Meryl has beaten it over the years very well. And I think Jack [Nicholson] has done well. He trusts himself in lots of situations and seems to be supportive even of lesser projects—with Bob Rafelson, let's say—where he's being loyal. He's not worried that it's the end of his career if he makes a mistake. It's that thing with stars that can drive you crazy. But you asked about actors, not stars. I've had very good success, but I believe it's because I'm prepared and at least make them think I know what I'm doing.

Katharine Hepburn always told the story of how she was having trouble playing Rosie in The African Queen ***until John Huston told her, "It's Mrs. Roosevelt."***

When you come up with the right thing like that, it's a miracle, and it's great directing. That's a great direction. Once I hear it, it's wonderful.

It can be something that specific.

Yes. Frank Schaffner, who directed me in a two-hour television show about the Brink's robbery, and Frank was a fabulous guy, a polite, talented, wonderful gentleman. He would just walk by you during the rehearsal period and whisper in your ear, "He's cold." Something. It was helpful. That's all he would ever do. He would never say, "Let me explain the scene to you." You don't want to do that with actors. They're smart people. You only want to say something if they need help.

And you can tell?

I've used other tricks and techniques. They're not secrets. I've studied the works of Michael Chekhov, who's written a wonderful book, *To the Actor*,[61] I would recommend that to all would-be actors and directors, where he uses a lot of tricks and things, like you play your character as if he were an animal. What animal is your character? So you say, "He's a rabbit," and you think of yourself as a rabbit [*Mazursky becomes a rabbit, pulling his hands up like paws and wiggling his nose*] and you are, you are, you are, you like to chew, and you have a hopping gate, you look around, you're a rabbit. You're an accountant and you're a rabbit, whatever it is. Now, the British actors don't need any of it. They're playing moment to moment and they're just good. Who knows? But when you see acting and it's not very good, you notice everything you weren't meant to notice—like the script.

---

61 *To the Actor on the Technique of Acting*, NY: Harper & Brothers, 1953

How much easier is it for audiences to like a character if they're laughing?

I can't answer anything like that. I can't speak for an audience. The only thing I can say about an audience is that, even though they often have terrible taste, or else why would so many of the things we see are popular be popular, they also have a nose for the truth. When something wonderful comes and, they recognize it. It's all a question of how many people recognize it, how big that audience is. If you can adapt Proust, you're not going to have a vast audience. You're just not. I don't know how Mel Brooks wrote *Blazing Saddles* or how the guys wrote it with him, but it was hilarious. And I know that when the studio first saw it, they hated it. They were distraught—"Where can we burn this?"—until they showed it. You've got to have some judgment about what's funny to have Alex Karras punching a horse in the mouth. They didn't know. They're sitting in the screening room alone, four executives, and they're worried.

Is there such a thing as a cheap laugh?

Yes. When Mel Brooks has six guys around a campfire farting, it's a cheap laugh. But it's funny, and they did it.

What other screenwriters have influenced you?

Preston Sturges. Billy Wilder, I.A.L. Diamond, John Huston, Alvin Sargent's very good, Robert Bolt, there's quite a few others that are not coming to me. Frank Pierson; he's very solid. He did a wonderful job on *Dog Day Afternoon*, a film I was offered at one point and probably should have made. William Goldman can certainly write, although I'm so afraid of being killed by William Goldman if I say something bad, because he's very funny and he's a master, but some of the things he does are not as important—I don't know why. Bob Towne; *Chinatown* is terrific.

What makes these scripts good?

They come alive on the page. By the way, I haven't read the scripts to most of them, I only read the ones I was offered. I was offered—maybe not a guaranteed offer—but I was shown *All the President's Men* by William Goldman. Fabulous! This moron [*indicating himself*] didn't do it because I was writing *Next Stop, Greenwich Village* and I wanted to finish my movie and then do it. But it was a great script. What makes them good? I don't know. You just see the movie and they know what they're doing and they're talented. I read the scripts that I wrote and the ones I've been offered. I've read very few others.

In your scripts, there's a consistency of character—you don't bend things so that the scene ends a certain way. Everything flows from the character.

A lot of the scenes I've written are used in acting classes. I get calls from people that they're using *An Unmarried Woman*, stuff like that. I've also never been afraid of long scenes, whereas now the style is to be very brief and very fast and lots of cuts, and the dialogue, you know, you get a half a page of dialogue and you're on to the next. They get very nervous. So I would write long and complicated things where they're talking about things that maybe other people wouldn't talk about. I do use certain tricks that I like. I like emotional encounters that take place in public places. I like a guy breaking down and telling his wife on a busy street corner, "I'm cheating, I'm having an affair. I met her at Bloomingdale's. I was buying a shirt and she was standing right next to me. She's a school teacher. She asked me a question." I like those encounters in front of people. I have them in many movies I've done. I like it when they talk about curiously banal things at very emotional moments: "my shoes hurt," or whatever it is. I've had discussions of things you don't have many discussions about in movies any more like, "Should the Rosenbergs go to jail?" in *Next Stop*, or T.S. Elliott, or they're making references to things that, if you stop and look, the studio won't want it because the focus group won't know who you're talking about, et cetera. That self-censorship keeps you from writing good stuff. The good writers I've talked about—Frank Pierson, Bob Towne, William Goldman—I don't think they care about that either. The audience can usually get something even though they may not know what it is. They understand that you're onto something. If you get too erudite it gets pretentious, but if it's about people, it won't. In *Next Stop, Greenwich Village* these people are trying desperately to be *avant-garde* and with-it and political and all that. Right now it's different. They talk more about rave parties and Ecstasy and IPOs. I don't know what young people talk about now, which is why I'm probably not the kind of guy to write a script about very young people.

Have you ever come up with an idea which is a great idea but it's not a Paul Mazursky film?

I don't come up with that many great ideas. I don't know what a "Paul Mazursky film" is. I know what people always think when they talk about my movies: "he makes those movies about the humanistic middle class, you know, with social problems and with humor—*Bob & Carol, Blume in Love, Down and Out in Beverly Hills.*" But then I went out and made *Moon Over Parador* which is a satire about dictatorships and actors, there's *Enemies, A Love Story* which is a domestic drama. I've made a few different ones. What I've never made is an out-and-out thriller. It might have been fun to have made one.

Do you think that the filmmakers that we accuse of being "artistic" are trying to make art, or are they making what, to them, is entertaining and interesting and everybody else regards it as art.

They're all different. There are a few who are trying to make art—Tarkovsky. Art with a capitol "A." The pan will take an hour, just the pan. Antonioni. Ar-tis-tic. When they work on both levels it's fantastic.

Look at your friend Fellini. Half a dozen of his films are among the greatest statements ever made.

They're very entertaining too. *Amarcord* is hilarious. And even though it's a downer, *La Strada* is overwhelming. Ah, but Fellini's another story. He also did some essays on film; he's one of the few famous filmmakers who did that: *Roma, Clowns, Orchestra Rehearsal*. They're not like normal feature films. Then there's *Intervista* where he visits Anita Ekberg and Mastroianni, and he's making a movie and he's in it, too.

When you started making films, directors were considered artists. Now they're just the guys who make the films. I can remember when there were academic seminars held about "Who's funnier: Mel Brooks, Woody Allen, or Paul Mazursky?"

Mel Brooks is a combination of many things. He's surprising. When I had my bypass five years ago he was one of the first people to call me. [Does Brooks] "How are you! You're a national treasure! Don't leave us! Don't go! Did it hurt?" He came over to the house and he was crying. "Mel!" "Paul!" Hug. You see, Fox in the 70s was a miracle place. You've got to understand. They were making movies and the following people were either in residence or making movies there: Mel Brooks, Paul Mazursky, Bob Altman, Bob Fosse, [and also Mark Rydell, Stanley Donen, Irwin Allen, James Bridges, Peter Bogdanovich, and Robert Aldrich]. We were all there. Alan Ladd, Jr. was the guy responsible in many ways. I gave Alan Ladd, Jr. *Next Stop, Greenwich Village* to read on a Thursday or Friday and he okayed it on a Saturday. *He said yes in one day!* For that movie to be made today would require a meeting of the Senate committee! It would be like getting approval for a nuclear attack. Alan Ladd, Jr. had giant balls. Those balls should probably be in an institution. They're not around any more. Now most decisions are based on, "Look, we can get Jim Carrey, we can get so-and-so, we can get Adam Sandler. It'll open big." Whatever it is. And they do.

After all of this, do you still like writing?

Well, I haven't written anything in the last few months, so I shouldn't say I like it. I sure like the *idea* of writing. It's the most difficult thing, in many ways. But when I've written well, it's come out pretty good. It's hard. And I may be at that age when I get a lot of ideas but I don't finish them. I have notes on a variety of things. I have a movie idea about a sculptor who is about sixty, becomes obsessed with the fact that people he doesn't think that much of are just starting to die and are getting these fantastic obituaries. He doesn't understand why because they're not really that good. And he starts to obsess on his own obituary. And he starts to reach the point where he wants to read his own obituary. Does it exist? And he finds out, of course, *The New York Times* has his obituary already written, but he can't read it, and so he gets even more obsessed. He starts to develop this ploy and he gets to read it. And, by God, it's not nearly as good as some of the others. I won't tell you the rest. It's interesting. Then I'm working on an idea right now with David Freeman, based on something I read in the newspapers. We'll see what happens.

Do you ever send your old stuff around again, figuring that studio heads have rolled since the last time they went out, so you've got another shot?

Yes. I got the script *Nirvana* that Leon and I wrote which is about a Larry King-Johnny Carson, big time talk show host, slightly younger, who gets annoyed. His marriages are all screwed up, he's very successful, he's a playboy, and he develops heart trouble and high blood pressure he goes away to an ashram called Nirvana. A physical place. And he falls in love with his yoga teacher who doesn't like men any more, but she's got a ten-year-old son, and something great happens out of it. It's very funny. We wrote it for Touchstone. They never did it, and it's been sitting there four or five years now. I read it again not long ago, and I've got these new managers, and I said, "Just read this." They said, "It's fabulous." So they're trying to sell it. We'll see what happens.

EPILOGUE

Something struck me as I was going over these conversations for this book after twenty years of remembering them: Paul didn't just talk, he listened. His responses reacted to my specific questions. They weren't canned responses, and this created a dynamic which—as happens when actors bond during a scene—lifted the level of both performances.

Yet despite the congeniality of our conversations and the unguarded honesty of his responses, something was missing. Something ineffable. Although I think he respected me for doing my research, I was never able to feel as close to Paul the man as I did to his films. Perhaps this was because I can be an aggressive interviewer—I will push if I sense there's more to an answer than my subject is giving me, or if I've read the answer elsewhere—and this may have put him off, especially if he was used to other interviewers who function more as stenographers. This hit me profoundly after we'd finished our talks and I asked him to sign my copy of his 1999 autobiography, *Show Me the Magic*. He wrote, "For Nat, Thanks for a splendid interview! Paul Mazursky." Handing it back, he said, without further comment, "I never give personal inscriptions."

This, from the greatest personal filmmaker of his generation.

And yet he sort of did, didn't he?

Some time later, when the cut-down version was published by the University of California press in *Backstory 4* in 2006, I sought him out at the Farmer's Market in Los Angeles where he and his friends hung out every morning. I made a show in front of them of handing him the book. He thanked me, set it down on the table, and went back to talking with them. He didn't pass it around while I was there, nor did he invite me to join them. I thought that was strange until, years later, when I spoke to a fellow journalist who had also extensively interviewed him. I told him my experience and he agreed that he had also been just as surprised to find Paul so distant.

I was reluctant to discuss this here, but I think it needs to be considered. When people say "judge the art, not the artist," they're usually talking about ogres like Pablo Picasso, Richard Wagner, Michael Jackson, Bill Cosby, Patricia Highsmith, or J.K. Rowling.

Paul, of course, was nothing like any of them. His contradictions were, in my opinion, more personal and tragic, for they were directed solely at himself. Go back and look and you'll see that a tinge of bitterness hovers above his memories, especially the later ones. He hides it with humor but the shading is unmistakable. When he was writing and directing his own material, he channeled bitterness into the tone of his work, letting his characters, as his proxies, hash it out with Life. When he stopped directing his own scripts, however—that is, his last twenty-one years—he had no way to express himself so freely, and I sensed, looking back, that this emerged in the way he dismissed his disappointments in the Q&A. He backhanded them, but he really didn't.

Paul was a sensitive, creative, caring man who, I feel, became a cynic when he could no longer fully apply his immense gifts. Had such projects as *Down and Out in Beverly Hills 2: Broke, Moscow on the Rocks,* and other later scripts (see Appendix B) come to fruition, would he have been less bitter? Or was there something in his creative mojo that needed to be poised at the edge of a personal abyss?

We'll never know, of course. Whatever his eyes saw when they looked inside, when they looked outside they saw a world of richly drawn characters navigating human foibles while bringing the audience along for an ennobling, emotional ride. Paul Mazursky's characters always wound up back on their feet. I wonder if Paul ever did.

Paul died on June 30, 2016 of cardiopulmonary arrest. His wife, Betsy, died September 29, 2017. They are survived by their daughter, producer-writer Jill Mazursky. Their daughter Meg Mazursky died in 2009.

AFTERWORD: Jill Mazursky

Jill Mazursky, born in 1965, is the younger daughter of Paul and Betsy Mazursky. Her older sister, Meg, died in 2009. Married to Steve Cody, with whom she has two children, Molly and Tommy, the couple is now separated. A writer and producer, she now produces high-end documentaries for a variety of venues and lives with her aggressively friendly white Samoyed dog, Dingo. Jill is very much her father's daughter. Not only does she look like him, she has a stealth, sharp wit tempered by his warm personality, all while being very much her own person. This interview took place September 7, 2021 at the completion of this book.

Nat Segaloff: *I'm going to start by asking the most banal question possible: What was it like living in a Beverly Hills home with one of the world's great filmmakers?*

Jill Mazursky: When I was about to go into kindergarten. My dad called Fellini[62] and Fellini said, "if you're ever in Rome, look me up" and my dad came home and said, "Honey, we're moving to Rome." My sister, who was eight years older than me, was in seventh grade. I didn't go to kindergarten, I went to the American school in Rome, but I really hated it so I didn't go every day. Then when we got back and lived in Hancock Park, everybody there who entered grade school had already met each other, so it was pretty hard for me to make friends.

My dad was pretty eccentric; he was the only one who had ethnic friends, hippie friends, there were VW vans in front of our

---

62 Mazursky and Fellini had become friends when the maestro made an appearance in *Alex in Wonderland*.

house, which was a very WASPy, conservative neighborhood. We stuck out; we were the only Jews. This was fifty years ago (my mom wasn't Jewish buy my dad was). It was difficult. I mean, my parents had a friend who was a hunchback and he drove a sports car.

By the time I was in fourth and fifth grade I got into movies and was very, very close to my dad. My mom wasn't into it. My dad would say, "Warren Beatty wants us to come over for a party tonight" and she would say, "what time?" and he would say, "seven-thirty" and she would say, "that's too late." So I was his plus-one many, many times.

So you really did grow up in a Fellini movie.

Yes, and the other thing that was interesting is that, once I did make friends, and I didn't have a ton of friends, all my friends wanted to be at my house. My parents were second parents to my friends. There would be five of us here every day waiting for my father to come home at five or six o'clock, and he would sit down and tell us about his day and he was the best storyteller. We would just sit around and laugh our asses off. My dad knew everybody, but in terms of the people who would hang around the house, it was regular people -- with big personalities.

Tell me about your mom, because I know your dad absolutely loved her, and other people did, too.

My mom was very funny but very quiet and never was your typical Hollywood wife. She never went to Neiman-Marcus. She never got her nails done professionally. She didn't like to drive, she didn't like to fly, she sort of did her own thing and was very low-key. They were both Depression-era so they saved everything.

When people came over did she do the Jewish thing and bring out cake and tea?

No, she would bring out leftovers and they were pretty disgusting. She wasn't a big cook; very eccentric. I used to joke that she did Medieval cooking: she would throw roots and potatoes in the oven and do nothing.

Tell me about your sister Meg. Was she enamored of show business?

She was older than me. We lived in Hancock Park, like I said, and then we decided to move to Beverly Hills so we could go to better public schools, because my parents were big public school people. My sister didn't want to go to Beverly; she'd been going to Fairfax High School and she went to the Krishna Murti boarding school in London for her senior year. She was a vegetarian and into yoga and very, very pretty. Had a lot of boyfriends. Went to Bard College. She got married very young to a guy named Jeb and had kids when she was in her early twenties. She was into casting for a little but, but after she had her kids she stayed home. She was more like my mom and I was like my dad; she would butt heads with my dad a little bit because he was such a jokester. He was a great father and would do anything for us.

When you shot on distant locations did the whole family come along? Like shooting Tempest on the Greek islands?

My sister definitely went to Greece. We always threatened to do a tell-all book about it. It was crazy. I was sixteen so my sister was twenty-three. She probably had her kids right after that. It was Susan Sarandon, Raul Julia, the Cassavettes clan, Nick [Cassavettes] was there and we were isolated and people were trying to find pot and having affairs. It was one of the movies where a lot of shit happens. Then we were in Brazil for *Moon Over Parador*, but my sister didn't go for that. I was there with a friend. And Sammy Davis, Jr. would show up with his luggage, which was like twenty-five Louis Vuitton cases, and Jonathan Winters. My dad would always cast his friends; Andre Philippe and Michael Greene were his two best friends.

When he made Yippee![63] it was a kind of homecoming for him, wasn't it?

Yes, and he reunited with Jeff Kanew[64] who kind of helped him put it together. He didn't want to stop working until the day he died. His last years were insane; I had to sort of run the show. No matter what horrible thing was going on with him, with dialysis or getting his leg amputated or being in a wheelchair, he wanted to see everything. Every friggin' foreign movie. I took him to see *Waiting for Godot* with two major actors downtown. He's begging me. I get him into the theatre. He passes out immediately and wakes up an hour and a half later, "that was amazing!" I was having housekeepers take him to the Laemmle because he didn't want to miss some Swedish movie.

So he had his wits about him all along.

Yeah!

Did he have black hair all the way through to the end?

Pretty much.

Your father's films of the 1970s and 80s are a chronicle of the flaws of the middle class done with love, but still showing the flaws. Did your father see his own flaws?

He definitely used stuff that was going on in our lives. My sister, who was very skinny, was the girl in *Down and Out in Beverly Hills*. I was the boy! *The Pickle* was our family, and also *Next Stop, Greenwich Village*.

He wrote sequels to Down and Out and Moscow on the Hudson and he couldn't get them made. I mean, he put Touchstone

---

63 Paul visits Uman, a small Ukrainian town which, each year, hosts 25,000 mostly Hasidic Jews.
64 Jeff Kanew is a major producer of trailers for the industry.

Pictures on the map and they wouldn't make his movie. When I asked him about it, all I got was a shrug.

He would be disappointed but he would always move on. He was a great pitcher. He could go into a room and tell a story and people would want him to write it. Then sometimes they would let him do the movie, and sometimes they wouldn't.

Is there anything you would like the world to know about your parents that I haven't asked?

I feel I was so lucky, and I still miss them. They're not replaceable. They were unique and generous and I wish more people were like my parents. My dad was really a mensch, and you don't run into that many people who are like my dad.

Appendix A:
Paul Mazursky Filmography (non-acting)

"The Tinhorn" (*The Rifleman*, TV, 1963; story, co-script)
"From Cara With Love" (*The Cara Williams Show*, TV, 1964, co-script)
"Dog Watch" (*The Cara Williams Show*, TV, 1964, co-script)
"Cara's Private War Against Poverty" (*The Cara Williams Show*, TV, 1965, co-script)
The Danny Kaye Show (TV, 1962-1966, writing staff)
Last Year at Malibu (1961, short, co-everything)
The Monkees (TV, 1966, pilot co-script)
What's Up, Tiger Lily? (1966, Woody Allen; uncredited contribution)
I Love You, Alice B. Toklas (Hy Averback, 1968, co-script)
Bob & Carol & Ted & Alice (1969, co-script)
Alex in Wonderland (1970, co-script)
Blume in Love (1973, script)
Harry & Tonto (1974, co-script)
Next Stop, Greenwich Village (1976, script)
An Unmarried Woman (1978, script)
Willie and Phil (1980, script)
Tempest (1982, co-script)
Moscow on the Hudson (1984, co-script)
Down and Out in Beverly Hills (1986, co-script)
Moon Over Parador (1988, co-script)
Enemies, A Love Story (1989, co-script)
Taking Care of Business (1990; executive produced only)
Scenes from a Mall (1991, co-script)
The Pickle (1993, script)
Faithful (1996, directed only)
Winchell (1998, TV, directed only)
"Big Shot's Funeral: Paul Mazursky in Beijing" (2001; documentary short)
Coast to Coast (2003, TV, directed only)
Yippee: A Toast to Jewish Joy (2006, documentary, directed and co-produced)

Appendix B: Unrealized projects:

H-Bomb Beach Party! (1965, co-script)
Uncle Sam's Wild West Show (1971; co-producer)
Hallelujah, Hallelujah (1974; co-script)
Down and Out in Beverly Hills 2: Broke (1987, co-script)
Moscow on the Rocks (1992, co-script)
Pictures of Fidelman (1994, co-script)
Poor (1995, co-script)
My Friend, the Messiah (1995, 1995, co-script)
Heart of a Dog (1996, co-script)
Freddy Faust (1998, co-script)

Since *Bob & Carol & Ted & Alice*, Mazursky functioned as producer on the films he wrote and directed. These appendices do not include his many acting roles.

Autobiography: *Show Me the Magic* (NY: Simon & Schuster, 1999)

Appendix C: Notable Awards:

Academy Award® nominations; screenplay: *Bob & Carol & Ted & Alice; Harry & Tonto; An Unmarried Woman; Enemies, A Love Story;* picture: *An Unmarried Woman;* commendation for service to Board of Governors;

Writers Guild of America nominations; screenplay: *Blume in Love; Harry & Tonto; Next Stop, Greenwich Village; An Unmarried Woman; Down & Out in Beverly Hills; I Love You, Alice B. Toklas!;* Best Episode, Music Variety Show: *Danny Kaye Show, December 2, 1962; Danny Kaye Show, February 3, 1965;*

National Academy of Television Arts & Sciences; commendations: *Writing Emmy® Awards Show, 1963-4; Emmy® Awards Show, 1965-6;*

Prix Femina Belge du Cinema, Diplome d'Honeur, *Harry & Tonto*

Hollywood Foreign Press Association Golden Globe Award Nomination, screenplay: *Down & Out in Beverly Hills; Harry & Tonto*

Los Angeles Film Critics Association: Best Screenplay, *An Unmarried Woman;*

New York Society of Film Critics: Best Film, *An Unmarried Woman*

New York Film Critics Circle: Best Screenplay, Picture: *An Unmarried Woman;*

New York Film Critics Circle: Best Director: *Enemies, A Love Story*

Greenwich Village Chamber of Commerce: Commendation for *Next Stop, Greenwich Village*

Brooklyn College, Distinguished Alumnus Award

NAT SEGALOFF Biography

Nat Segaloff is a writer-producer-journalist. He has variously been a studio publicist, college teacher, broadcaster, and newspaperman. He is the author of over twenty books including *Hurricane Billy: The Stormy Life and Films of William Friedkin*, *Arthur Penn: American Director* (now in a second edition from BearManor Media), and *Final Cuts: The Last Films of 50 Great Directors* in addition to career monographs on Stirling Silliphant, Walon Green, John Milius, and Paul Mazursky (of which this book is an expanded and updated iteration). His writing has appeared in such varied periodicals as *Film Comment, Written By, International Documentary, Animation Magazine, The Christian Science Monitor, Time Out* (US), *MacWorld*, and *American Movie Classics Magazine*. He was also senior reviewer for AudiobookCafe.com and contributing writer to *Moving Pictures* magazine. His *The Everything® Etiquette Book* and *The Everything Trivia Book* and *The Everything® Tall Tales, Legends & Outrageous Lies Book* were published by Adams Media Corp.

Nat is the co-author (with Daniel M. Kimmel and Arnie Reisman) of *The Waldorf Conference*, a play about the secret meeting of studio moguls that began the Hollywood Blacklist, which had its all-star world premiere at L.A. Theatre Works. and was acquired for production by Warner Bros. He was staff producer for The Africa Channel, wrote the stage comedy *Closets* (produced at Massachusetts' Gloucester Stage Company), and was writer for the popular public radio quiz show "Says You!" after having been a frequent guest panelist.

Other books include *A Lit Fuse: The Provocative Life of Harlan Ellison* (NESFA Press), nominated for Hugo and Locus awards, and, for Bear Manor Media, *Stirling Silliphant: The Fingers of God*; *Mr. Huston/Mr. North: Life, Death, and the Making of John Huston's Last Film*; *Screen Saver: Private Stories of Public Hollywood* and its sequel, *Screen Saver Too: Hollywood Strikes Back*, *Guiding Royalty: My Adventure with Elizabeth Taylor and Richard Burton* (co-written with Yoram Ben-Ami), *Guarding Gable*. More recently for Bear Manor he wrote *Big Bad John: The John Milius Interviews*, *Hollywood & Venal*, a collection of "stories with a secret" originally written for Nikki Finke's celebrated Hollywood Dementia® website (illustrated by Thomas Warming), and the second edition of *Arthur Penn: American Director*.

Nat lives in Los Angeles waiting for his phone calls to be returned.

Index

A

Abbott, Scott 158, 159
Academy of Motion Picture Arts and Sciences 57, 116, 197
Aiello, Danny 12, 152, 154, 155
Alex in Wonderland 12, 21, 23, 24, 17, 29-30, 55, 91, 138, 139
Allen, Woody 12, 13, 20, 22, 149-152, 151, 174, 183, 195
Altman, Robert 35, 60, 68, 183
An Unmarried Woman 16, 30, 47, 51-55, 61, 63, 65-66, 93, 97, 156, 160, 167
Anspach, Susan 47
Antonioni, Michelangelo 38, 182
Arden, Eve 173
Arkin, Alan 73
Aubrey, James 35, 36
Averback, Hy 12, 195

B

Baker, Lenny 18, 61, 63
Baryshnikov, Mikhail 101
Baskin, Carol 101-103
Bates, Alan 66, 68, 70, 73, 74, 121
Beatty, Warren 178, 190
Benedek, Barbara 172
Benjamin, Richard 31
Benyami-nov 103
Beresford, Bruce 96
Berghof, Herbert 64
Bergman, Ingmar 81, 96, 103, 174
Bierce, Ambrose 155
Bissell, Jim 156
Blacklist 80, 199
Blauner, Steve 24
Blume in Love 24, 30-35, 39, 62, 82, 97, 126, 130, 133, 157, 168

Bob & Carol & Ted & Alice 12, 15, 18, 20, 23, 24, 29, 31,32, 35,44, 60, 93, 97, 132, 150, 161, 168
Bogdanovich. Peter 60, 183
Bovasso, Julie 88
Braga, Sonia 130, 134
Brando, Marlon 177
Bridges, James 183
Brody, Adrian 167
Brooks, Richard 11, 13, 22, 180, 183
Brubeck, Dave 62
Buñuel, Luis 86, 106, 129
Burstyn. Ellen 52, 53, 120

C

Caan, James 31
Cacoyanis, Michael 92
Calley, John 45, 58
Cameron, James 87
Canby, Vincent 33
Cannon, Dyan 26, 29-32, 57, 116, 117, 156
Capetanos, Leon 17, 44, 89, 94, 117, 126, 175
Carney, Art 12, 55-57, 60, 172
Carrey, Jim 183
Carson, Johnny 184
Cassavetes, John 34, 90, 93, 94, 95, 98, 119,191
Chagall, Marc 36
Chaplin, Charles 109
Chayefsky, Paddy 170
Chekhov, Anton 179
Cher 156, 157
Chopra, Depak 46
Chung, Connie 101
Cinecittà Studios, Rome 98
Clayburgh, Jill 66, 67, 72, 75, 77, 115, 117, 121, 122

Cody, Iron-Eyes 72, 91, 113, 189
Columbia Pictures 12, 32, 33, 35, 68, 91, 104, 153
Condit, Gary 48
Conti, Bill 160
Coppola, Francis Ford 99
Corliss, Richard 33
Cosby, Bill 186
Culp 26, 29-31, 34, 116, 156

D

Danny Kaye Show, The 11, 16-18, 20-22, 42
Davis, Sammy Jr. 129, 191
DeCorti, Espera 58 (n), 72
DeLaurentiis, Dino 39, 174
DiMaggio, Joe 71, 93
Down & Out in Beverly Hills 46, 75, 90, 91, 93-95, 97, 111, 125, 160, 168, 172, 178
Dreyfuss, Lorin 125, 127
Dreyfuss, Richard 11, 12, 23, 31, 33, 105, 106, 108-111, 112, 125, 130-132, 134, 135, 143, 167, 172, 196, 200
Dumont, Margaret 23
Dunne, Griffin 156

E

Ebb, Fred 97 (n)
Edelman, Julius (Skippy) 17
Egan, Michael 64
Eisner, Michael 105, 140, 149, 150, 175
Ekberg, Anita 183
Enemies, a Love Story 2, 43, 56, 119, 123-138, 157, 168

F

Faithful 16, 139, 142, 143
Fargas, Antonio 62
Fauchois, Rene 110

Fellini, Federico 13, 37, 39, 43, 63, 96, 182, 183, 189, 190
Fields, Freddie 7, 31
Fine, Sylvia 9
Fitzgerald, Geraldine 54, 55
Flaksman, Marcos 112
Florey, Robert 125
Fonda, Jane 68
Fosse, Bob 183
Frankovich, Mike 12, 31, 32, 35

G

Gabler, Neal 160
Gabriel, Gilbert 125 (n)
Gassman, Vittorio 90, 98
Gazzara, Ben 173
Gelbart, Larry 18
Gerson, Carlotta 134
Godfrey, Arthur 54
Goldblum, Goldblum 64
Goldman, William 180-182
Gould. Elliott 26, 30-32, 57, 116, 156, 172, 181
Greene, Michael 132, 191
Gudinov, Alexander 101
Guinan, Texas 161
Guzman, Pato 72-73, 89-91, 98, 103, 107, 126, 127, 133, 148, 150, 152, 166

H

Hagman, Larry 52
Harry & Tonto 1, 9, 24, 30, 31, 37-45, 51, 55, 71, 72, 79, 126, 156
Hartig, Herb 11, 17, 18, 59, 64
Harvey, Laurence 21
Haynes, George 62
Headley, Glenne 161
Highsmith, Patricia 186
Hitchcock, Alfred 169
Hitler, Adolf 161
Hoffman 55, 95, 101, 139

Holden, William 128
Holland, Agnieszka 129
Hopper, Hedda 161
Hughes, John 26
Huston, Anjelica 43, 123 (n), 125, 129, 158
Huston, John 165, 166

I

I Love You, Alice B. Toklas 4, 7, 11-13, 17, 29, 119 (n)

J

Jackson, Glenda 35
Jackson, Michael 172
Jacobellis, Nico 2
Jacobi, Lou 62
Jaffe, Stanley 68, 69
Jagger, Mick 89
Jarre, Maurice 131, 133, 143
Jenkins, Paul 74
Jews and Jewishness 9, 10, 16, 21, 61, 73, 74, 88, 109, 130, 137-139, 190, 195

K

Kael, Pauline 33, 61, 63
Kamins, Ken 2
Kander, John 97 (n)
Kanew, Jeff 192
Kanter, Jay 69
Karras, Alex 180
Kasdan, Lawrence 172
Kaye, Danny 11, 16-18, 20-22, 43, 195, 197
Kazan, Elia 90
Keller, Sheldon 18
Kellin, Mike 11, 62, 64
Kidder, Margot 79, 85, 117, 120
Kristofferson, Kris 47
Kubrick, Stanley 11, 97, 109

L

Ladd, Alan Jr. 53-55, 61, 63, 67-69, 91, 183
Laemmle, Carl 192
"Last Year at Malibu" 18
Lauder, Harry 54
Levy-Gardner-Laven 17
Leyda, Jay 16
Lindsay, John 32
Lucken, Kimberly 2, 13

M

Mahareeshi Maheesh Yogi 46
Malamud, Bernard 166, 167
Marr, Sally 56
Marx Bros. 23
Mastroianni, Marcello 183
Mazursky, Betsy Purdy 11, 23, 29, 30, 37, 38, 63, 94, 95, 113, 115, 119, 121-123, 186, 189
Mazursky, Jill 2, 7, 11, 26, 66, 67, 70, 72, 73, 75-77, 113, 115, 117, 121, 122, 187, 189, 191, 193
Mazursky, Meg 173, 175, 177
Mazursky, Paul (see also film titles) 1-4, 6-16, 18, 20, 22-26, 28-30, 32-34, 36, 38, 40, 42-44, 46, 48-52, 54, 56-58, 60-64, 66, 68, 70, 72, 74, 76-80, 82-84, 86, 88-90, 92-94, 96, 98, 100, 102, 104, 106, 108, 110, 112-126, 128, 130, 132-138, 140, 142, 144, 146, 148-150, 152, 154, 156, 158, 160, 162-164, 166, 168-170, 172, 174, 176-180, 182-196, 198-200, 202
McAlpine, Don 89, 90, 96, 99
McGuane, Thomas 85
McKee, Robert 168
Medavoy, Mike 38
Midler 105, 108, 109, 149, 172
Miller, Barry 154
Monkees, The 3, 10-1, 17, 24, 25, 195
Montagu, Ivor 16
Montgomery, Robert 18

Moon Over Parador 19, 61, 72, 97, 111, 112-119, 168, 177
Moreau Jeanne 38, 79
Moscow on the Hudson 61, 73-75, 77, 85, 88-90, 97, 124, 139, 172, 178
Mostel, Zero 52, 53

N

Next Stop, Greenwich Village 1, 30, 42-52, 66, 97,126, 134,140, 167-169, 178
Newman, Paul 175
Nicholson, Jack 156, 172, 178
Nolte, Nick 104, 172
Nykvist, Sven 81, 96

O

Ontkean, Michael 12, 79, 83
Oscar® 2, 32, 33, 50, 55, 97, 116
O'Connell, Arthur 173
O'Neal, Ryan 156

P

Palminteri, Chazz 156, 158
Pappé, Stuart 35, 76
Parsons, Louella 161
Patinkin, Mandy 85
Picasso, Pablo 186
Pierson, Frank 180, 182
Pickle, The 90, 116, 138-142, 178
Plummer, Christopher 161
Pollack, Tom 131, 132, 135
Preminger, Otto 173
Price, Frank 91, 102, 104, 126, 153, 156

R

Rafelson, Bob 24, 178
Rand, Ayn (see Alisa Zinovyevna Rosenbaum)
Reagan, Ronald 112, 131, 135
Reisz, Karel 16, 147

Reitman, Ivan 132
Remmick, Lee 173
Renoir, Jean 105, 110, 112
Ringwald, Molly 70, 90
Ritzlin, Jeremy (Jerry) 2, 31
Rosenbaum, Alisa Zinovyevna, 99
Roth, Joe 16, 141-143
Rotunno, Giuseppe 96
Runyon, Damon 160
Rowlands, Gena 90, 94, 95, 98

S

Sackler, Howard 11, 62
Sandler, Adam 183
Sarandon 90, 94, 98, 191
Sargent, Alvin 180
Scenes From a Mall 126, 134-135
Schaffner, Franklyn J. 179
Schickel, Richard 33
Schneider, Bert 24
Schreiber, Liev 167
Scorsese, Martin 60, 99, 160
Seeger, Linda 168, 171
Segal, George 12, 16, 46, 47, 49, 50, 62, 144, 172
Sellers, Peter 12, 22, 26, 27, 162
Sharkey, Ray 79, 85, 88
Sheedy, Ally 156
Silver, Ron 70, 137, 143, 144
Simon, John 47
Simon, Michel 91, 92
Simon, Neil 8, 9
Simon, Roger L. 30, 124, 126, 138, 151, 152
Singer, Isaac Bashevis 123, 124, 126, 128, 132,
Stein, Margaret Sophie 137, 139, 143
Stiller, Jerry 154
Streep, Meryl 85, 149
Stromberg, Hunt 21
Sturges, Preston 142, 152, 180

T

Taking Care of Business 12
Tamiroff, Akim 125
Tecolote Productions 13
Tempest 75-79, 82, 83, 85, 90, 97, 122, 139, 179
Thomas, Danny 35, 200
Tinhorn, The 3(n)
Tolkin, Mel 18
Travolta, John 155
Truffaut, François 25, 39, 83, 84
Tucci, Stanley 159, 162
Tucker, Larry 11, 17-21, 23-26, 31, 32, 34, 36, 37, 43, 44, 52, 58, 63-65, 165, 172, 175, 184

W

Walken, Christopher 62
Wallace, Mike 160
Welles, Orson 9
Weston, Jay 39
What's Up, Tiger Lily? 6
Wigan, Gareth 67, 69
Wilder, Billy 84, 180
Williams, Robin 12, 17, 100, 101, 103, 172, 195
Willie and Phil 30, 65-74, 85, 97, 126
Winchell 26, 144-147
Winchell, Walter 9, 40, 158-161, 195
Winogradaff, Anatole 56
Winters, Shelley 11, 62-64, 154
Woodward, Joanne 175

Y

Yippee 178

Z

Zinnemann, Fred 68

www.ingramcontent.com/pod-product-compliance
Lightning Source LLC
Chambersburg PA
CBHW051925160426
43198CB00012B/2040